Trina Hankins

GOD'S HEALING WORD

A Practical Guide to Receiving Divine Healing

Unless otherwise indicated, all scripture quotations are taken from the King James Version of the Bible.

God's Healing Word
First Edition 2013

Published By
Mark Hankins Ministries
PO Box 12863
Alexandria, LA 71315
www.markhankins.org

ISBN: 978-1-889981-43-7
Spiral Bound

Printed in the United States of America.

TABLE OF CONTENTS

Foreward

It has been with joyful anticipation that I have looked forward to the printing of Trina's book, *God's Healing Word*. The declarations spoken from the mouth of God are, "I am the Lord that heals you. I sent my word to heal you and to deliver you from your destructions." (Exodus 15:26 and Psalm 107:20)

In order for the gift of God's healing words to be complete, they must be received with a grateful heart. The words penned in this book are coming to you from the heart of one who has proven her Father God faithful and His promises to be true. She is a living testimony of God's compassion to heal and to make whole.

As you read and contemplate these writings, your faith will come alive and your hope will soar, causing you to believe and to "see" yourself well and your health restored. Your God will say to you, "My child, what you see is true and I want you to know that I am active and alert and I am watching over my Word to make it happen. You are the believer and I am the performer."

This hope He gives you is your joyful, confident expectation of God's promises being fulfilled in your life. Your hope is the picture of God's promise painted on the canvas of your mind through which you reach out with a hand of faith, making it yours.

In joy fully,
Ginger Behrman
Trina's Mother

God's Healing Word is a perfect prescription for anyone with a challenge of sickness. We read about this medicine in Proverbs 4:20-22, ***"My son, give attention to my words; Incline your ear to my sayings. Do not let them depart from your eyes; Keep them in the midst of your heart; For they are life to those who find them, And health to all their flesh."*** In these verses it is clear that God's healing word is taken through your eyes and ears and your meditation, which involves your thoughts and words. The useful and practical instruction in this book is not only the product of diligent study, but is also the proven divine medicine that saved Trina's life. As her little sister, I always looked up to Trina and was influenced by her "show and tell" example in many areas. I've been especially inspired to watch her actually take God's Word as medicine and the last word on her health. Trina's testimony of the powerful effect of God's healing Word is not exclusive to her but an exhibit of what God's Word will do for anyone who takes it!

This was an old song that we sang as a family:

I will sing of my Redeemer
and His wondrous love to me
On the cruel cross He suffered
From the curse to set me free.

I will praise my dear redeemer
His triumphant power I'll tell
How the victory He gives
Over sin and death and hell.

I will sing of my Redeemer
With His blood He purchased me.
On the cross He sealed my pardon
Paid the debt and made me free!

Trina's story and song has always been and still is of her Redeemer. I'm forever grateful that she helped teach me redemption's healing song so I can sing it myself!

–Patsy Cameneti
Trina's Sister

SECTION ONE:

How to Receive Divine Healing

Every year billions of dollars are poured into health care and yet people are still suffering. The parking areas surrounding hospitals and medical facilities are full as people crowd into waiting rooms for hours to see a doctor. There are drop–in clinics and drive–through pharmacies providing more convenience for customers. There are new therapies, drugs, treatments and surgeries to repair, remove, or replace whatever is broken. People set their clocks and arrange their schedules so they can take their medicine because it cost them $500! Yet, some are never healed.

This is nothing new. In fact, thousands of years ago there was a healing balm found in a place called Gilead, where people would travel great distances in order to be healed. "Gilead" means a perpetual spring and in this place grew a certain kind of tree from which the healing balm was taken. People would come up to Gilead sick and broken, and along the way, they would meet others coming back from the healing waters with new life and energy. Yet, some were not healed there because they rejected God, who is the Great Physician. They didn't take the healing medicine.

When Jesus began to teach, He was overwhelmed by the masses of people who pressed in to touch Him and to be healed. Jesus gave hope to those who had given up on medicine. There were some who came to hear and be healed. The Greek word for healing used many times is *therepeuo* and means "to relieve of disease, cure, heal and worship." The people were not just curious or just going to "try this and see if it works." No, they came and took in Jesus' words. They worshiped Him as God, expecting to receive as they acted upon what He said. This was Divine Therapy and they received Divine Healing.

In this book, *God's Healing Word,* you will find testimonies of how many people, including myself, have been healed as we not only believed in divine healing, but took God's healing word as medicine. There is a healing balm found in the leaves of the Word of God for anyone who will simply meditate and receive the therapy. It is free for all because the price has been paid in full and the doctor is always in.

"IT APPEARS THAT YOU HAVE AN INOPERABLE BRAIN TUMOR,"

the radiologist said as he read the report from the CAT scan done on my brain after I was admitted into the emergency room. But before his words registered on my consciousness, I heard the voice of the Living God on the inside. Like a shield of faith and a fountain of refreshing water, the Word of God surrounded my mind. "He sent His Word and healed them...Himself took our infirmities and bore our sicknesses...the strong spirit of man will sustain his infirmity." These were scriptures I had learned and meditated on for years beginning as a teenager. They had penetrated my heart and now that Word was more real to me than anything the doctor was saying! Let me tell you the story.

He sent his word, and healed them, and delivered them from their destructions.

- Psalm 107:20

CHAPTER ONE

He Sent His Word to Heal You

THE POWER OF THE WORD

All my life I had struggled with my health. Allergies and asthma were almost a daily happening. Mama and Daddy did everything they could—we tried allergy shots, distasteful medicine, breathing treatments and much prayer, too. On many nights, Daddy held me in the chair and prayed until we both fell asleep.

The church I was brought up in believed in the power of divine healing and praying for the sick. Responding to messages on healing was something I was used to doing. The only thing was that I was unsure of how to "get my healing." I thought I might feel it or if I begged and cried, God might come through for me. I became discouraged and just about gave up on the healing thing. At about the age of sixteen, something happened that sparked a ray of hope.

One afternoon, my sisters and I sat down on our bed to listen to a preacher on a cassette tape. Spellbound, we listened as he preached about the redemptive work of Christ on the cross. I always believed in what Jesus did, but now I learned more. I found out how He was made to be a curse on the cross for us and that the curse Jesus broke included not only spiritual death, but also sickness.

That afternoon, my sisters and I started shouting when we understood how Jesus took that curse for us on the cross and defeated Satan. He reclaimed the keys of authority and gave them to the Church (Matt. 18:18,19). Jesus gave us the authority and the right to use His name.

I have a part to play in receiving my healing.

This meant that I was free from the curse of asthma and it wasn't God who was making me sick. The truth of John 10:10 dawned on me: "The thief (the devil) cometh not but for to steal, and to kill and to destroy: but I (Jesus) am come that they might have life, and that they might have it more abundantly."

I began to see that healing is something already purchased and provided for me by Jesus on the cross, and through faith I could receive it. I didn't have to get it, but Jesus already got it for me. Thank God, that day I found out God sent His Word to heal me.

He sent his word, and healed them, and delivered them from their destructions.

Psalm 107:20

That's when I discovered that I have a part to play in receiving my healing. My faith seemed so small and I struggled so much—but now there was hope! Jesus said that the Word of God is a seed (Mark 4:3-20). A natural seed has to be planted and watered to cause it to begin to sprout and grow. In the same way, the seed of divine healing can be planted in your heart by hearing and believing what the Bible says about it. Next, it must be watered by acknowledging it out loud through meditation and praise. When I understood that, I realized that the seed of God's Word would grow to produce healing in my body.

Isaiah 53:4, 5 was especially liberating to me. I learned and became convinced that Jesus not only bore my sin, but also every sickness and pain. As I studied, I saw that when Jesus was whipped and wounded, He actually "lifted" every sickness and disease from humanity with every blow that He took (see page 145).

Surely He has borne our griefs (sicknesses, weaknesses, and distresses) and carried our sorrows and pains [of punishment], yet we [ignorantly] considered Him stricken, smitten, and afflicted by God [as if with leprosy]. But He was wounded for our transgressions, He was bruised for our guilt and iniquities; the

3

chastisement [needful to obtain] peace and
well-being for us was upon Him, and with the
stripes [that wounded] Him we are healed and
made whole.

Isaiah 53:4, 5 (AMP)

When Jesus took our sin and sickness, He bore them away and removed them. As our substitute, Jesus absorbed our griefs, sorrows, sickness, and pain. Galatians 3:13 says that Jesus actually became a curse for us on the cross. That led me to study what the curse of the law included. The curse is found in Deuteronomy 28 and lists every category of sickness and disease.

God's plan of redemption included physical healing as well as spiritual regeneration. In God's mind, Jesus' death, burial and resurrection was restoring man's spirit, soul and body to wholeness.

Psalm 119:130 (NKJV) says, "The entrance of Your words gives light...." That's exactly what was happening for me. I saw my asthma, along with emotional distress, being lifted off of me 2,000 years ago when Jesus bore them on the cross.

I had a collection of healing scriptures and confessions that I would meditate on every day (these are the same scriptures that are in this book). Since breathing was such a struggle some nights, sitting up was the only way to get air. That's when I would get those scriptures out.

4

I would start at the beginning and go to the end, speaking them out loud and letting the image of divine healing be imprinted in my mind and heart. It would take almost an hour, but relief would come. I would take my asthma medicine and then God's medicine! Proverbs 4:20-22 says this about God's Word: "My son, attend to my words; incline thine ear unto my sayings. Let them not depart from thine eyes; keep them in the midst of thine heart. For they are life unto those that find them, and health to all their flesh." I praised, I cried, I sang, I laughed, and I danced! I did my best to act on the Word. All the time the seed of faith for healing was growing.

FAITH HAS AN ATTITUDE

Fear and self pity are major negative factors when sickness and disease are present, but they can be displaced with faith and confidence. Some may enjoy the attention they get when they're sick or may have just given up on being well, deciding there's no hope. You have to make a decision that you really want to be healed. Jesus asked the crippled man by the pool of Bethesda in John 5:6 in the Amplified, "Do you want to become well? [Are you really in earnest about getting well?]" This man had given up on getting into the healing waters and had a very negative attitude, even feeling sorry for himself. Jesus didn't pamper the man, but commanded him to act in faith and to get up. Here was the Healer Himself standing in front of him. The man had a quick change of attitude and got up, healed.

In Luke 13, there was a woman who was bowed over and couldn't stand up straight. Jesus commanded her to be loosed from a spirit of infirmity. She wasn't demon possessed, but that demon had attached itself to her body. The moment Jesus commanded the spirit of infirmity to go, her body was released and the woman stood up straight. He spoke with boldness and authority and demons recognized it. Not all sickness is caused by a demon, but in this case it was. Remember there was no sickness, disease, or dysfunction of any kind until Adam sinned. Jesus came on the scene and demonstrated how believers can use their authority and release the anointing to heal. It is the thief who has come to steal, kill and destroy, but Jesus came to give abundant life!

> *Fear and self pity are major negative factors when sickness and disease are present, but they can be displaced with faith and confidence.*

Faith has an attitude of boldness and because of the Word, I was getting that attitude! One night when awakened by an asthma attack, a "holy anger" against it arose in my heart. I'd had enough! I heard the Holy Spirit on the inside prompt me to resist the spirit of infirmity out loud and command it to go! James 4:7 says, "...resist the devil and he will flee from you." First Peter 5:9 says to resist him steadfast in the faith. I was acting on Mark

11:22-23, speaking TO the mountain of sickness. The Holy Spirit showed me this was a spirit of infirmity and now I had boldness to take a stand against it. I shouted, "I resist you, spirit of infirmity! Get out of my body in the name of Jesus!" I began to praise and worship God with all my heart. That night my health began to improve until asthma became only a memory of the past.

Through meditation on the Word concerning healing, my life was revolutionized. It gave me a strong conviction that healing was God's will. I became like the wise man who built his house on the rock. When the storm came, his house stood firm.

Being grounded upon this "rock" of healing held me through a dreadful storm soon to come. Some people are like the man who had a hole in his roof and didn't see the need to fix it because it wasn't raining. When it did begin to rain, it was too late—he had waited too long and couldn't fix it. Don't wait until you need healing to get grounded in faith for healing. Instead, build your faith up so that when an evil day comes, you will stand, and keep standing (Eph. 6:13).

THE "EVIL" DAY

On Sunday evening, July 7, 1991, I left the church service with a severe headache. A few minutes later, I suffered a seizure. Thankfully, there were doctors and others in the medical profession in church that night who acted quickly to get help.

Once at the hospital, many tests and MRI's were done and the diagnosis was an inoperable brain tumor. My husband, Mark, took a stand on the Word and decided not to fear, but to only believe. He posted a sign outside my hospital room door which said, **"No Wavering Allowed."** Next, he placed a tough lady outside of my door with a list of people who were allowed in the room. Only those with a strong spirit of faith could enter.

> *Faith has an attitude of boldness!*

In times of crisis, it really does make a difference the company of people you spend time with. You need to be surrounded with people who will encourage you to trust God. It will determine if you have victory or defeat. Only a few people were admitted into my hospital room—people of strong faith. When you are feeling sick you are more sensitive to negative attitudes of the people around you. Sympathy, though well-meaning, is detrimental to your faith and can even kill you! Jesus Himself had to put certain people out of the room to keep faith in the room (Mark 5:40)! You don't need sympathy—you need support!

From Monday through Friday many tests were run, tears cried, battles fought and praises sung. I'm forever grateful to my family and friends who prayed fervently and praised God with strength. Sometimes we'd get a guitar and start singing songs about the power of the Word to heal. If it wasn't time to sleep, it was time to speak the Word or to praise God. The TV stayed off and all conversations were filled with faith in God. We were in the fight of faith and that's no time for goofing off!

> *Sympathy, though well—meaning, is detrimental to your faith and can even kill you!*

THE FIGHT TO FOCUS

Numbers 21:1-9 tells the story about Moses leading the Jews in the wilderness. They were complaining about the menu of manna and talking about how hard their lives were. Because of their attitudes, poisonous snakes started biting them until they cried out for help from Moses. When he prayed about what to do, God told him to make a brass serpent and put it on a pole. When the people would look at it, they'd live and not die. Think about the effort it took to look away from the snakes and focus on the brass serpent. Snakes were crawling everywhere, biting everyone except those who kept looking at that pole. Imagine the frantic struggle parents had as they screamed to their children, "Don't look at the snakes! Only look up and you will live!" That is the seriousness of keeping your focus on the Word. Look at it, keep saying it and you will live.

9

The Amplified Bible says in Numbers 21:9 that when anyone looked, *"attentively, expectantly, with a steady and absorbing gaze,"* they lived. Their hope and expectation were focused only on the brass serpent, which was a type of Jesus being lifted up on the cross. That's exactly what we did in that hospital room for five days. We kept our focus on the Bible which fed our faith. Our expectation was on God alone.

> *My soul, wait thou only upon God; for my expectation is from him.*
>
> *Psalm 62:5*

Friday came and preparations were made for a surgery to determine if the tumor was cancerous. My husband was briefed concerning the complications that could result from this surgery and warned of possible paralysis or other brain damage. From the medical perspective, the future looked bleak as they presented the possibilities of more experimental surgery in Atlanta or Dallas. Thank God for the shield of faith! Those words of the doctors never penetrated my consciousness or moved us from a place of confidence in God.

THE POWER OF JOY

God is the performer and we are the believers. After 25 years and trying to get a miracle their own way, Abraham praised God until his faith was strong (Romans

4:20) and Sarah's laugh of disbelief changed to a laugh of faith (Genesis 21:6; Hebrews 11:11). Together, they received their promised son and called him Isaac, which means laughter.

My hospital room was full of praising and joy because we wanted to stay full of faith. My nurse told me later that she was amazed to come into the room and see our faith in action. God inhabits our praises—it is the atmosphere for miracles to happen. There was peace in my mind and a joy from the inside that came bubbling up. That laughter was the joy of the Lord. I remember lying on the bed, being wheeled down to surgery, laughing at the contraption they had fastened to my head to assist them in the surgery. I had no fear or dread, only peace. There's something big in a little laughter. It does good like a medicine.

> *A merry heart doeth good like a medicine:*
> *but a broken spirit drieth the bones.*
>
> > *Proverbs 17:22*
>
> *A glad heart makes a healthy body....*
>
> > *Basic*
>
> *A glad heart is excellent medicine, a spirit*
> *depressed wastes the bones away.*
>
> > *JER*

Job 5:22 says, "At destruction and famine thou shalt laugh...." I believe at this very moment, the Holy

Spirit began a supernatural operation! He is the power that raised Christ from the dead and is the One who confirms the Word with signs following and brings joy unspeakable, full of glory! The glory is the manifested power of God that destroyed the works of the devil! 1 John 3:8 says, "... for this purpose the Son of God was manifested, that he might destroy the works of the devil." The word "destroy" in this verse is *luo*, which means: to destroy, loosen and dissolve; a meltdown. **The power of God can destroy any work of Satan.** That's what Jesus was doing in Acts 10:38, "How God anointed Jesus of Nazareth with the Holy Ghost and power and, who went about doing good and healing all who were oppressed of the devil, for God was with him." I believe that joy and laughter released the power of the Holy Spirit to do an operation of a different kind!

> *Joy and laughter release the power of the Holy Spirit to do an operation of a different kind.*

HEALED BY THE POWER OF GOD

After hours of waiting through the operation, Mark was met by a pleased but puzzled doctor. He said they had thoroughly and repeatedly explored for the tumor, but it was no longer there! We had a medical confirmation of a spiritual operation! I returned home after a few days to recover from the effects of the surgery, including slight paralysis. Each day of recovery had its struggles, but there was an assurance that what God had started, He would finish. The Word continued to be the central focus of my attention and Mark helped me keep the Word and praise in my mouth!

> *Our part is to believe and God's part is to do the miracle.*

A few weeks after the healing, Bro. Kenneth E. Hagin gave us some very valuable advice. He said that many times healing is lost in a counterattack and that we needed to hold fast to what God had done. This fight involved casting down imaginations such as thoughts of a recurrence and permanent paralysis caused by the operation itself. **The good news is that the Holy Spirit will stick with you until the battle is completely finished!** Again, He sent a Word just in time. Nahum 1:9 in the Amplified Bible is what we began to rejoice about. It says, *"...He will make a full end...the affliction shall not rise up the second time."*

STAY IN A POSITION OF FAITH

In Mark 5, we see the story of the woman who was healed from the issue of blood. When she heard about Jesus, she got up and pressed her way through the crowd and touched Him. Instead of staying home and remaining sick, she decided that day to begin a journey that changed her life forever. These are the four steps of faith she took.

1. She said, "If I can touch Jesus, I know I'll be healed."
2. She did. She touched Jesus' clothes.
3. She felt the power or virtue of Christ flow into her body.
4. She told about it (she testified).

I identified with her and as I read her story in the book of Mark, something stood out to me. After she touched Jesus and told Him her story, He said these words to her: "Daughter, your faith...has restored you to health. Go in (into) peace and be continually healed and freed from your [distressing bodily] disease," Mark 5:34, AMP. The Holy Spirit said to me, "Trina, stay in the position of faith, which is a position of rest." My part is to believe and God's part is to do the miracle. When you believe, you come to a place where your mind is settled and at peace and your attention is thoroughly fixed on God's faithfulness and ability.

> *Healing is a process,*
> *supernatural from beginning to end.*

Many times in Jesus' ministry, people were healed as they went. I had experienced a miracle and now I needed to stay in a position of faith and rest until I was completely restored and off all medications. Healing is a process, supernatural from beginning to end. I found the peace of God is not passive, but active. Philippians 4:7 in

14

the Amplified Bible says, peace will "garrison and mount guard over your hearts and minds."

Divine healing was received into my spirit and from there it affected my body. God's peace is a spiritual force and it guarded my mind, will and emotions, fighting the battle for me. To this day, I am healed and made whole, continually experiencing God's healing power and peace. I learned that the same faith that healed me will keep me well.

> *The same faith that made you*
> *whole will keep you whole.*

I pray that you will lay hold on the power of God's Word to heal you and that you will understand healing was purchased for you in the death, burial and resurrection of Christ. May you be restored to health by the power that raised Jesus from the dead. I encourage you to study the next chapters thoroughly. You will have a personal experience with God as you meditate upon His Word concerning health and healing. He sent His Word to heal you! There is hope in the Word of God no matter what your case may be.

Maybe the doctors or those around you have not given you any promise of recovery. Maybe it seems your life cannot change. I want to offer you hope in God's Word. Grasp this promise given to us from Jeremiah

30:17 (AMP): "For I will restore health to you, and I will heal your wounds." The Message Bible says it this way, "As for you, I'll come with healing, curing the incurable, Because they all gave up on you and dismissed you as hopeless."

> *Beloved, I pray that you may prosper in all things and be in health, just as your soul prospers.*
>
> *3 John 2 (NKJV)*

MEDITATION POINT:
He sent his word, and healed them, and delivered them from their destructions. Psalm 107:20

ACTION POINT:

_____

_____

_____

My son, attend to my words; incline thine ear unto my sayings. Let them not depart from thine eyes; keep them in the midst of thine heart. For they are life unto those that find them, and health to all their flesh.

- Proverbs 4:20-22

CHAPTER TWO

Biblical Meditation— God's Medication

HOW TO MEDITATE

Have you ever found yourself mentally creating an entire scenario about something dreadful happening? Soon you have worked yourself up into a frenzied state of mind with your blood pressure elevated and your heart racing. That is the result of meditating on the wrong thing. We see the effects of wrong thinking, but just imagine the power of thinking on God's Word or His thoughts. Jeremiah put it this way:

> *Your words were found, and I ate them, And Your word was to me the joy and rejoicing of my heart.*
> *- Jeremiah 15:16 (NKJV)*

> *When your words showed up, I ate them - swallowed them whole. What a feast!*
> *MSG*

When your words came, I devoured them.

JER

Your words are what sustained me, they are food to my soul.

Taylor

The dictionary defines the word *meditate* as this: to talk with yourself, mutter, cogitate. It is an inward and outward conversation. To meditate means to study, chew, think over, ponder, excogitate, muse, reflect, mull over and speculate. Cogitate means to think deeply, think out, think up, dream up, and to hatch. Excogitate is to invent or create mentally. Christian meditation is NOT sitting on the floor with your legs crossed, humming to yourself and emptying your mind. It is a relationship with the Word of God. If you know how to worry or if you have been offended, then you know how to meditate in a negative way. You think about what could happen, what is happening, and speculate about the results. Worry even affects your body and emotions!

Christian meditation is a relationship with the Word of God.

David mastered the art of meditating upon what he referred to as the "law of the Lord." Psalm 1 captures the delight, discipline and the blessing that follows a person who meditates day and night on God's Word. The result of this lifestyle is this: "He shall be like a tree planted by the rivers of water, that brings forth its fruit in its season, whose leaf also shall not wither; and whatever he does shall prosper," Psalm 1:3, 4, NKJV. The Hebrew word for *meditate* in verse 2 is "hagah."

The Spirit-Filled Life Bible has this note: ***Hagah represents something quite unlike the English "meditation," which may be a mental exercise only. In Hebrew thought, to meditate upon the Scriptures is to quietly repeat them in a soft, droning sound, while utterly abandoning outside distractions. From this tradition comes a specialized type of Jewish prayer called "davening," that is reciting texts, praying intense prayers, or getting lost in communion with God while bowing or rocking back and forth. Evidently this dynamic form of meditation-prayer goes back to David's time.*** [1]

Meditation can be compared to eating. My mother–in–law was the slowest eater I knew. We would start our meal together and two hours later she would still be chewing. She would tell me the benefits of eating slowly. Doctors say you should chew your food 32 times before swallowing and that digestion begins in your mouth where the food is broken down before you swallow. God's Word is meant to be eaten and it is faith food. "Man shall not live by bread alone, but by every word that proceedeth out of the mouth of God," Matthew 4:4.

21

Faith comes by hearing and hearing by the Word of God (Rom. 10:17) and it has to be digested to be effective. When a child first feeds himself, he might have food in his hair or all over the floor, however only the food that gets in his mouth and is swallowed is what nourishes him. When you meditate on God's healing medicine, the Word gets into your eyes, your ears, and your mouth. Once it gets in your mouth you'll begin to digest it. This is when it brings health to all your body.

TAKE GOD'S MEDICINE

My son attend to my words; incline thine ear unto my sayings. Let them not depart from thine eyes; keep them in the midst of thine heart. For they are life to those that find them, and health to all their flesh.

Proverbs 4:20-22

...I, the Lord, am thy physician.

Exodus 15:26 (Leeser)

The medicine God prescribes is His Word. Many make the mistake of substituting their belief in healing for the actual taking of God's medicine—His Word. They say, "I believe in healing," without actually taking the medicine. What good would it do you to believe in water if you didn't actually drink any? You would die of thirst.

THE WORD OF GOD IS MEDICINE

God is the Great Physician and has prescribed His

Word as medicine for your healing. His Word has been proven to heal, but must be taken according to directions.

God's Word is a healing agent, just as natural medicine is a healing agent or catalyst. There are several parallels between God's medicine and natural medicine. In other words, the medicine itself contains the capacity to produce healing. God's Word contains within it the capacity, the energy, the ability, and the nature to effect healing in your body. Psalm 107:20 says, "He sent his word, and healed them, and delivered them from their destructions." Fenton's translation says, "He sent out His Word, and it healed, and from their corruptions it freed!" Proverbs 4:22 says, "For they (God's Words) are life to those that find them and health to all their flesh."

> *God's Word contains within it the capacity, the energy, the ability, and the nature to effect healing in your body.*

There are four simple steps that extract the power contained in God's Word and will bring healing and a cure to anything.

1. FEED ON GOD'S WORD

Isaiah 55:10, 11 says the Word will accomplish what it was sent out to do. The Word itself contains the power to produce what it says. Just as when God said in Genesis, "Let there be light," there was light. Healing scriptures contain within them the capacity to produce healing. Hebrews 4:12 says, "The Word of God is quick, and powerful, and sharper than any two–edged sword, piercing even to the dividing asunder of soul and spirit...." Weymouth's translation says, "God's message is full of life and power...." Jordan's translation says, "God's word is alive with energy...." **The key to partaking of the life and healing energy in the Word is feeding on it until it penetrates your spirit where it activates that life and energy.**

2. RECEIVE HEALING

We might say medicine is no respecter of persons; it will carry out its assignment in the body of any individual that takes it. However, the way each person's body receives it affects its ability to heal. **It is not a matter of whether or not God is willing to heal an individual, but whether or not the individual will receive healing by faith.** We receive healing by taking the medicine that produces faith. God's medicine works for anyone that takes it!

3. USE ACCORDING TO DIRECTIONS

Most importantly, **medicine must be taken according to directions to be effective.** Some medicine labels read "take internally," others say, "use externally." To rub it on your body externally when the directions say to take it internally will not work. To take it after meals when the directions say to take it before meals will reduce its effectiveness. To take it once in a while when the directions say three times every day will mean limited results, if any. No matter how good the medicine is, it must be taken according to directions, or it will not work. So it is with God's medicine, His Word.

God's prescription is found in Proverbs 4:20, 21: "My son, attend to my words; incline thine ear unto my sayings. Let them not depart from thine eyes; keep them in the midst of thine heart." Attending to His Words, inclining your ear to them, and keeping them before your eyes causes them to get into the midst of your heart.

Notice that it is only as God's Word abides in the midst of your heart that it produces healing in your body. Head knowledge won't do it. His Word has to penetrate into your spirit through meditation (attending, hearing, looking, muttering, musing, and pondering) to produce healing in your body. But once His Words do penetrate, they will surely bring health to all your flesh. Proverbs 4:20 in The Living Bible says, "...let them penetrate deep within your heart."

You can see again that God's way of healing is spiritual. Power is ministered first to your spirit; it works in your soul (your mind, will and emotions) and then is distributed to your body. God's medicine must be taken internally. In Mark 4, Jesus compared the Word of God to seeds that must be planted in the ground of your heart. Like a natural seed, once it is planted, it needs water so it will sprout, grow and develop fruit.

4. *GIVE GOD'S MEDICINE TIME TO WORK*

We also must remember that it takes time for medicine to work. Most people pay a high price for medication and give it a lot of time to work. They are diligent about it. They don't just take one dose and stop. Do the same with God's medicine: keep taking it and give it time to work.

Listen, instead of wondering whether you have enough faith to be healed, just take the medicine. This book includes a list of healing scriptures—feed on them several times a days, repeating them over and over again to yourself. Instead of picturing yourself weak, sick or dying, begin painting a picture on the canvas of your mind of healthy cells, bones, blood and organs. See yourself living life to the fullest and doing things any healthy person can do. It's wonderful to listen to others speaking or singing the Word of God, but nothing can substitute for you personally opening your mouth to speak or sing God's

Word. God's medicine will work if you will get it inside of you.

> *It doesn't matter what the problem is—God's Word is just the medicine you need!*

Use it in praise to the Father. It doesn't matter what the problem is—God's Word is just the medicine you need!

THE POWER OF MEDITATION IN ACTION

You may ask, "How can I apply this when I'm in pain and my situation looks hopeless?" I encourage you to read the following wonderful stories of healing and see the results of meditating on the Word of God.

DR. LILIAN B. YEOMANS: SUPERNATURAL HEALING

Dr. Lilian B. Yeomans, a medical doctor and surgeon, received divine healing after becoming ill to the point of death due to a narcotic addiction. She heard of Jesus' healing power in Mark 5:25-34 and was restored to fellowship with God and to health. She and her sister later opened what they called a "faith home." Three or four sick people at a time would come and stay so they could be healed by God's divine power through faith in His Word.

One woman was brought to her home in an ambulance, dying from tuberculosis. She was taken to one of the bedrooms where Dr. Yeomans began ministering the Word to her.

27

Dr. Yeomans related: "I sat by the bedside and read to her from the Bible. I said to her, "Close your eyes and rest and just listen to the Word." And for two hours Dr. Yeomans read healing scriptures, like the ones contained in this book. Instead of giving this woman a shot to stimulate her heart, she gave her a dose of God's medicine—His Word! She didn't read any scriptures other than the ones on the topic of healing, which was what she needed.

Dr. Yeomans related: "I had read to her the entire chapter of Deuteronomy 28 and Galatians 3. Then I read other healing scriptures, but I re-read these two chapters to her over and over again.

Then I asked her, "Did you notice that according to Deuteronomy 28:22, that consumption, or tuberculosis, is a curse of the law? But did you also notice that according to Galatians 3:13, Christ has redeemed us from the curse of the Law? Therefore, He has redeemed you from tuberculosis."

In those days tuberculosis was one of the biggest causes of death in America. That was before the days of miracle drugs and advanced medical technology. This woman was in the last stages of the disease and was virtually dead as she lay there on the bed in that faith home.

Dr. Yeomans instructed the woman, "At every waking moment, repeat out loud, 'According to Deuteronomy 28:22, consumption or tuberculosis is a curse of the Law. But according to Galatians 3:13, Christ has redeemed me from the curse of the Law. So Christ has redeemed me from tuberculosis.'"

The next morning, Dr. Yeomans asked the woman, "Did you say what I told you to say last night?"

"Yes," the woman answered. "It seems like I didn't even sleep ten minutes; I must have said it ten thousand times. But it still doesn't mean a thing in the world to me."

"That's alright," Dr. Yeomans said, "just keep saying it...." The woman with tuberculosis continued to take God's medicine. When Dr. Yeomans went to her room to read to her the next morning, she asked the woman, "Are you saying what I told you to say?"

"Yes," the woman answered. "It seems like I didn't sleep but ten minutes last night. I must have quoted those scriptures ten thousand times. But they still don't mean a thing to me. I don't feel like I'm getting anything out of it."

Afterward, Dr. Yeomans and her sister were in the kitchen cooking the noon meal when they heard some commotion upstairs in one of the bedrooms. It sounded like somebody had hit the floor and was running. All of the patients had been bedfast and virtually dead, but one of them was up, out of bed and running. And she was calling, "Dr. Yeomans! Did you know I'm healed? I'm healed! I'm the one who had tuberculosis, but I'm healed!"

"Yes, I know it!" Dr. Yeomans replied. "I've been trying to tell you that for almost three days now." [2]

What happened to this woman who was dying just days before? The Word she had been confessing got down into her spirit. It wasn't some magic potion that Dr. Yeomans gave her. And it wasn't Dr. Yeomans' great personality or abilities bestowed on her by God that got that woman healed. No, it was just the Word! It was simply faith in God's Word that healed the woman and raised her off her deathbed.

DR. DAVID YONGGI CHO:
HOW TO SUBDUE SICKNESS

Dr. David Yonggi Cho teaches about receiving healing through meditation. He calls man's spirit the fourth dimension, through which Christians can develop their faith and subdue the natural realm, which comes through our five senses. He has developed his spirit through many hours of daily prayer and through meditation upon the redemptive work of Christ. Then, based upon the teaching of Jesus in Mark 11:23, he teaches that believers must speak in order to release their faith. Cho teaches four distinct Christian spiritual disciplines that can bring all God's promises into reality: **1)** Thinking on God's Word; **2)** Meditation (or in Dr. Cho's words: visions and dreams); **3)** Faith and believing; **4)** Mouth speaking.

One particular time Dr. Cho needed healing and he took 1 Peter 2:24 as his healing medicine. He got a handheld counter and clicked it each time he spoke this scripture out loud to himself. He counted one thousand times he said this verse. Dr. Cho tells how he completely saturated his mind with the water of the Word of God. His mind and body became so thoroughly filled with the water of the Word that when he spoke, he released blessing and his body was healed. [3]

DR. A.B. SIMPSON: *A HEALED HEART CONDITION*

Dr. A.B. Simpson, a minister who suffered a heart ailment, had heard and received Jesus, not only as Savior of his life spiritually, but as healer of his heart. He believed and received Christ as his healer and made a decision to trust Him alone. Dr. Simpson told that when he went to a retreat to speak, he shared that testimony with the congregation. Immediately following the service, his faith was tested when he decided to go along with a group on a hike up a nearby mountain. They had heard his testimony of faith in Christ as his healer and now he was challenged to demonstrate it. This is what happened when he began his hike:

> *And so I ascended that mountain. At first it seemed as if it would almost take my last breath. I felt all the old weakness and physical dread; I found I had in myself no more strength than ever. But over against my weakness and suffering I became conscious that there was another Presence. There was a Divine strength that reached out to me if I would have it, take it, claim it, hold it, and persevere in it. On one side there seemed to press upon me a weight of death, on the other an Infinite Life. And I became overwhelmed with the one, or uplifted with the other, just as I shrank or pressed forward, just as I feared or trusted; I seemed to walk between them and the one that I touched possessed me. The wolf and the Shepherd walked on either side, but the Blessed Shepherd did not let me turn away. I pressed closer, closer, closer, to His bosom and every step seemed stronger until when I reached that mountain top, I seemed to be at the gate of Heaven, and the world of*

weakness and fear was lying at my feet. Thank God, from that time I have had a new heart in this breast, literally as well as spiritually, and Christ has been its glorious life. [4]

Dr. Simpson said that when he kept his thoughts on the Healer, his Shepherd, he experienced life and strength, but when he became engaged in talking with his companions, his mind on the natural, he felt weakness and pain. Every time he set his mind back on the Shepherd he received strength. From that day on, he never suffered from the heart condition. He emphasized the importance of making a bold testimony of faith and then following through with action. That action included keeping his mind and his words connected with what he believed in his heart. Dr. Simpson said, ***"As I shall meet Thee in that day I take the Lord Jesus as my physical life, for all the needs of my body until all my life-work is done; and God helping me, I shall never doubt that He does so become my life and strength that from this moment, and will keep me under all circumstances until His blessed coming, and until all His will for me is perfectly fulfilled."***

These were Dr. Simpson's 7 points to walking in health.

1. **Be fully persuaded**
2. **Be fully assured of the will of God to heal you**
3. **Be careful to be right with God**
4. **Commit your body to Him and claim His promise of healing**

33

5. Act in faith

6. Be prepared for trials

7. Use your new strength for God's glory [4]

REV. KENNETH E. HAGIN: NOTHING IS IMPOSSIBLE

One of the most remarkable testimonies of healing through the power of God's Word is that of Rev. Kenneth E. Hagin. Born prematurely, he was presumed dead, but after detecting life, he was rescued and nursed to life. As a child, he was always ill, suffering the effects of a deformed heart. He never ran and played like the other children and at age 15 he became bedfast. It was during that time he died and his spirit descended to hell three times and he experienced the torments of that very real place. On the third time, he called out for Jesus to save him. Instantly, he received eternal life and revived. (For more details read *I Went To Hell* and *I Believe In Visions* by Kenneth E. Hagin)

In 1933, Kenneth Hagin laid in the bed, happy to be saved, and began to read from his grandmother's Bible. Since he thought he didn't have much time to live, he started in the New Testament. At first, he could only read for ten or fifteen minutes at a time before he grew too weak to focus or hold the Bible. As he kept on, he was able to read for an hour. People would try to get him to read the comics or other things, but he refused, thinking he didn't have much time to live. As he read, he came to Mark 11:23 and it captured his attention. He tried to get pastors to come to teach him, but they never came. Finally, he asked God to help him understand that receiving God's promise came as a result of believing God's promise. The following is an exerpt from Bro. Hagin's book, *I Believe in Visions.*

> *As Kenneth read through the Gospel of Matthew and into the Gospel of Mark, he came to the Scripture passage that would transform his life and become a cornerstone of his ministry.*
>
> *And Jesus answering saith unto them, "Have faith in God. For verily I say unto you, That whosoever shall say unto this mountain, Be thou removed, and be thou cast into the sea; and shall not doubt in his heart, but shall believe that those things which he saith shall come to pass; he shall have whatsoever he saith. Therefore I say unto you, What things soever ye desire, when ye pray, believe that ye receive them, and ye shall have them."*
> *Mark 11:22–24*
>
> *Kenneth was thankful for his salvation, but in Mark 11, he saw the possibility of receiving something more. Rev. Hagin later said, "The*

greatest desire of my heart was to be well and strong." As he read this passage, the whole room became engulfed in light, as if someone had just pulled the shades open on a bright summer day. And he sensed that same light abiding within him.

Of course Satan came immediately, convincing Kenneth that "what things soever ye desire" only applied to spiritual matters. The light of revelation about this scripture had been dimmed, but Kenneth was still intrigued by and drawn to this scripture. The incorruptible seed of God's Word had been sown into Kenneth's heart.

He said, "I saw exactly what that verse in Mark 11:24 meant. Until then, I was going to wait until I was actually healed before I believed I had received my healing. I was looking at my body and testing my heartbeat to see if I had been healed. But I saw that the verse says you have to believe when you pray. The having comes after the believing."

MIRACULOUSLY HEALED

Finally, Kenneth knew he had been healed. But then he had to act on it. On the outside the situation had not changed. He was still bedridden. He still could not move his legs. The only thing that had changed was the light of revelation Kenneth had on the inside.

36

The Holy Spirit said to him, "If you are healed, then you should be up and out of that bed." In agreement, Kenneth pushed himself into a sitting position, then used his hands to swing his legs off the bed one at a time. With the devil fighting him every step of the way, Kenneth began to proclaim that he was healed and that he would stand and walk. He slowly but surely worked his way into a standing position, grasping tightly the post of the bed that had held him for 16 long months.

After some initial dizziness, feeling started to come back to his legs. "It was like two million pins pricking me," Kenneth said. After a short time, the pain subsided and he began to walk around his room. He told no one about this but did it again the following morning.

The following morning in August 1934, Kenneth got out of bed, dressed himself, and joined his family at the breakfast table. [5]

THE OTHER SIDE OF YOUR STEP OF FAITH

Take a moment to consider the benefits to you and your family as you receive your healing. Your good health will give you energy and strength to live a productive life. There is a plan God has for you, a path for you to walk in, good deeds to do and blessings to receive.

The woman who pressed through the crowd to touch Jesus' clothes probably went home to enjoy her family. Peter's mother-in-law got up and served a meal to a house full of company after Jesus touched her. What if Bro. Hagin had not received faith to be healed and gotten out of bed that day? Because of his experience and teaching, countless people are now enjoying divine health.

What is on the other side of your step of faith? You too, can be healed, but it's not just about you only. You can enjoy life, be a testimony and serve your generation.

MEDITATION POINT:

My son, attend to my words; incline thine ear unto my sayings. Let them not depart from thine eyes; keep them in the midst of thine heart. For they are life unto those that find them, and health to all their flesh. Proverbs 4:20-22

ACTION POINT:

_____

_____

_____

End Notes
1. Hayford, Jack W. *Spirit-Filled Life Bible*
2. Hagin, Kenneth E. *Healing Scriptures*
3. Cho, Dr. David Yongii, *Dreams and Visions* DVD
4. Simpson, Rev. A.B. *Gospel of Healing*
5. Hagin, Kenneth E. *I Believe in Visions*

Praise is magnetism that causes God's power to fall and explode where you are.

- Phil Driscoll

CHAPTER THREE

~~~~~

Thanksgiving and Praise

He sent His word and healed them, And delivered them from their destructions. Oh, that men would give thanks to the Lord for His goodness, And for His wonderful works to the children of men! Let them sacrifice the sacrifices of thanksgiving, And declare His works with rejoicing.

Psalm 107:20-22 (NKJV)

In Luke 17, ten men, all joyfully marveling as they examined their new skin; now free from the horrible stench of the dreaded disease of leprosy, made their way up the road leading into the city. They were headed to find the priest who had given each one the diagnosis and identity of "unclean."

That day had begun as any other for these outcasts who never could escape the pain. The sores and loss of various parts of their bodies were the constant reminders of shame and hopelessness. Disfigured and lonely, the untouchable men had just experienced the compassion flowing from the man called Jesus. He had entered the invisible barrier surrounding them and had given them a command to show themselves to the priest. As they walked by faith to see the priest, the power of Jesus' spoken word began to cure their leprosy. Their skin was now new and as clean as a baby's skin. Their pace picked up to a run as they anticipated the reversal of the priest's judgment of death to one of *healed*.

If you were watching that day, you would have seen one of those men come to a stop, look down at his body and slowly turn around with tears streaming down his face. His gaze turned back to the man, Jesus. He had to tell Him, "Thank you." When the leper returned to Jesus and fell at His feet, this once tormented man looked up into the Healer's kind face. From his heart flowed an unstoppable stream of gratitude and thanksgiving, praising Jesus publicly for healing him. Then Jesus asked him, "Where are the nine? Were there not ten cleansed and only this Samaritan returned to praise God? Get up and go your way. Your faith has restored you to health," Luke 17:17-19.

I can just imagine how this man began shouting and praising as he told everyone around about what

Jesus did for him. His returning to thank Jesus opened his heart for more. This one man, an alien from the Jewish covenant, was the only grateful one and the only one who Jesus pronounced completely restored.

GRATITUDE OPENS THE DOOR OF YOUR HEART

Webster's 1828 Dictionary gives this definition for the word "gratitude":

> *An emotion of the heart, excited by a favor or benefit received; a sentiment of kindness or good will towards a benefactor; thankfulness. Gratitude is an agreeable emotion, consisting in or accompanied with good will to a benefactor, and a disposition to make a suitable return of benefits or services, or when no return can be made, with a desire to see the benefactor prosperous and happy. Gratitude is a virtue of the highest excellence, as it implies a feeling and generous heart, and a proper sense of duty.* [1]

Gratitude to God proceeds from a heart full of appreciation and then it overflows into your emotions and finds expression in words, praise and joy. It is the ingredient in thanksgiving that gives great pleasure to the giver. Gratitude is connected to praise or lauding, extolling and magnifying God's goodness, mercy and ability. It is

43

connected with the idea and the word *sacrifice*. In the Old Testament, many of the sacrifices were animals and were required to be perfect, the first and best the worshiper could bring. God always has taken notice of the kinds of sacrifices people offered. They had to be personal and in obedience, as in the case of David when he refused to let a king provide a sacrifice to God.

> *Then the king said to Araunah, No, but I will surely buy it from you for a price; nor will I offer burnt offerings to the Lord my God with that which costs me nothing. So David bought the threshing floor and the oxen for fifty shekels of silver.*
>
> *2 Samuel 24:24 (NKJV)*

When David offered that sacrifice, healing came to his land. He knew that only heartfelt, personal, and pure sacrifices were the kind God was looking for. It cost David much and therefore was valuable and acceptable to God.

Aren't you glad you don't have to bring an animal to church to sacrifice nowadays? Now there is something we bring that will bring healing and blessing. It is the sacrifice of praise and thanksgiving. We draw near to God, not by our good works, but by what God in Christ has done and is doing for us. By Jesus' blood and in His name released from our mouths, we can enter the very presence of God Almighty. One translation of Hebrews 4:16 says we can come boldly to the "throne of the Giver."

> *Therefore by Him let us continually offer the sacrifice of praise to God, that is, the fruit of our lips, giving thanks to His name.*
> *Hebrews 13:15 (NKJV)*

> *Our constant sacrifice to God should therefore be our songs of praise, faithful confession of His name with our lips.*
>
> *Cent.*

David said, "My voice shall you hear in the morning," Psalm 5:3. Again, in Psalm 119:171 he says, "My lips shall utter praise." The voice of thanksgiving, praise and worship will always precede and give way to a miracle. As my husband, Mark says, "Your voice is your address in the realm of the spirit."

I really like what I heard Phil Driscoll say: "Your praise is magnetism that causes God's power to fall and explode in your life." With your voice, you release the faith in your heart and the rivers of life–giving water. You personally tap into the supernatural, the realm of the spirit where all things are possible. Christ, the Anointed One, is in you. That power is released as you begin to speak out your heartfelt thanks and praise. Nothing can substitute for your voice—not a clap, dance, or run. So don't let anyone do your thanking and praising for you. Listening to a recording of someone else is good, but that still can't substitute for you taking time to personally offer that sacrifice of praise.

LIFT YOUR HANDS TO RECEIVE

Thus I will bless You while I live; I will lift up my hands in Your name.

Psalm 63:4 (NKJV)

Throughout Biblical worship, people lifted their hands to offer thanksgiving. The word "thanksgiving" in the Hebrew is *towdah* and means: an extension of the hand; adoration of God.[2] It is a demonstration of the offering of your very heart to God and He is looking for this particular kind of worship.

The sacrifice that honours me is a thankful heart. Obey me, and I, your God, will show my power to save.

Psalm 50:23 (CUVEK)

What is on the other side of your obedience to give a thanksgiving offering to God? It is the mighty power of God to save! The Greek word for "save" is sozo and means to deliver or protect, to heal, preserve, save (self), do well, be (make) whole.[3] Our part is to offer a sacrifice of thanksgiving from our heart and obey Him. God gives His promise here, to show His power to save.

The voice of thanksgiving, praise and worship will always precede and give way to a miracle.

One of the first manners a child should learn is how to say "thank you." Our Heavenly Father God teaches us

46

to have an attitude of gratitude and to express our thanks. After we ask from Him, we extend our hands to receive and along with that we say, "thank you." It's a very simple thing to receive when you consider that God is your Father and has a reputation for goodness and generosity. It is good to know He will do exactly what He said and He operates supernaturally. If you want to get God's attention, open your heart with gratitude for all He is and all He has done. Then expect miracles!

> **Out of the mouth of babes and nursing infants You have ordained strength, Because of Your enemies, That You may silence the enemy and the avenger.**
>
> **Psalm 8:2 (NKJV)**

Thanksgiving gives way to praise. Praise will still the enemy and bring power to heal you and deliver you. It is like a detergent that washes out doubt, purifies your faith and lays hold on the power of Heaven!

KEYS THAT OPEN HEAVEN'S POWER

Thanksgiving and praise are the keys to opening the gifts of healing and miracles. Notice the part that thanksgiving and praise had in these Bible miracles.

Thanksgiving Bring Deliverance

When my soul fainted within me, I remembered the Lord; And my prayer went up to You, Into Your holy

47

*temple. Those who regard worthless idols Forsake their own Mercy. But I will sacrifice to You with the **voice of thanksgiving**; I will pay what I have vowed. Salvation is of the Lord. So the Lord spoke to the fish, and it vomited Jonah onto dry land.*

Jonah 2:7-10 (NKJV)

Thanksgiving Releases Resurrection Power

*Then they took away the stone from the place where the dead man was lying. And Jesus lifted up His eyes and said, Father, **I thank You** that You have heard Me....Now when He had said these things, He cried with a loud voice, "Lazarus, come forth!" And he who had died came out....*

John 11:41, 43, 44 (NKJV)

Thanksgiving Brings Multiplication

*So He commanded the multitude to sit down on the ground. And He took the seven loaves and **gave thanks,** broke them and gave them to His disciples to set before them; and they set them before the multitude.*

Mark 8:6 (NKJV)

Thanksgiving Brings Victory and Great Wealth

So they rose early in the morning and went out into the Wilderness of Tekoa; and as they went out, Jehoshaphat stood and said, "Hear me, O Judah and you inhabitants of Jerusalem: Believe in the Lord your God, and you shall be established; believe His prophets, and you shall prosper." And when he had consulted with the people, he appointed those who should sing to the Lord, and who should praise the beauty of holiness, as they went out before the army and were saying: Praise the Lord, For His mercy endures forever. **Now when they began to sing and to praise,** *the Lord set ambushes against the people of Ammon, Moab, and Mount Seir, who had come against Judah; and they were defeated....When Jehoshaphat and his people came to take away their spoil, they found among them an abundance of valuables on the dead bodies, and precious jewelry, which they stripped off for themselves, more than they could carry away; and they were three days gathering the spoil because there was so much.*

2 Chronicles 20:20-22, 25 (NKJV)

Thanksgiving Brings Freedom and Salvation

But at midnight Paul and Silas were praying and **singing hymns** *to God, and the prisoners were listening to them. Suddenly there was a great earthquake, so that the foundations of the prison were shaken; and immediately all the doors were opened and everyones chains were loosed....So they said, "Believe on the Lord Jesus Christ, and you will be saved, you and your household."*

Acts 16:25, 26, 31 (NKJV)

49

In the same way, your thanksgiving and praise release resurrection power and bring great breakthrough, provision, victory and supernatural deliverance to your life.

> *Praise will still the enemy and bring power to heal you and deliver you.*

THE PRAISE CURE

God has tied Himself irrevocably to human cooperation in the work of redemption. He has made man's faith a determining factor in the execution of Divine purposes.
Lilian B. Yeomans

I love this classic example of the power of praise told by Dr. Lilian B. Yeomans in her book called *Healing From Heaven*. She tells how there was a missionary to China who had ministered fearlessly to a sister missionary with smallpox.

> *Then a very bad case of confluent smallpox (that was what it looked like to the doctors) came out on her, and she did not know what to do; so she asked the Lord, and He told her to sing and praise Him for His faithfulness to His Word. They isolated her and told her to lie quiet; but she said if she didn't praise God, the very stones would cry out. So she*

sang and sang and praised and praised. The doctor said he feared for her life, that the case was serious and awful complications threatened. But she praised and praised and sang and sang.

He said she was evidently delirious but that he had so little help that he couldn't restrain her—and she sang and sang and praised and praised. They told her that if by any chance she recovered, she would be disfigured for life—and she sang and praised louder than ever. They asked, "Why do you praise so much?" She answered, "Because I have so many pox on me. God shows me I must praise Him for each one separately." And she kept right at it.

The Lord had shown her a vision of two baskets, one containing her praising—half full and the other, in which was her testing— full. He told her that the praise basket must be filled so that it would out balance the other, so she kept at it. Her songs and shouts were so Spirit-filled that they were contagious, and the Christian nurses couldn't resist joining in; so they kept the place ringing. At last the Lord showed her that the praise basket was full and overflowing. She saw it sink and the testing basket rise in the air; and in a

51

moment, as it seemed, the eruption and all the attendant symptoms vanished, leaving no trace in the way of so much as a single scar.

Yes, the praise cure works every time. It is not unpleasant; rather it is delightful; the cost of it has been met for us by another, and it is available this moment to each of us.

Are you ready to begin it? The last clause of 1 Peter 1:8 tells us exactly how to begin: "Believing, ye rejoice with joy unspeakable and full of glory."

Just believe what God says that Jesus has done for you, body, soul, and spirit—think about it, talk about it, sing about it, shout about it, and the praise cure has begun. You are not to take it once a year but all the time. [4]

NO DISTANCE IN THE SPIRIT

While visiting my sister and her husband in Italy, my dad got a small scratch on his arm which turned into septicemia (blood poisoning). Mark and I were preaching in Europe at the time, so I flew to Rome and rushed to the hospital in time to see daddy on the verge of a coma, his kidneys failing. My mother, Patsy, Tony and I laid hands on him in that ICU room and prayed, commanding the infection to go and taking a position of authority over death. Dad's arm was more than double its normal size from the infection.

We put our trust in God as we left the hospital. At my sister's home that night, after praying in the Spirit for a season of time, the Holy Spirit prompted us to sing. My mother and I sat up in the bed and sang hymns until we came to a sense of peace and victory. The next day when we walked into ICU, daddy was sitting up looking like a new man. We said, "Dad, what happened to you?" He replied, "I felt like singing last night, so I started singing hymns until I got so loud, the nurse came and told me to be quiet because I was disturbing the peace." That sounds like a praise service like Paul and Silas had in Acts 16.

Thank God for the power of praise and thanksgiving. Those songs of praise opened the door to the healing power from Heaven and broke the spirit of death. From that night, dad began to amend. It took some time but he regained all his health.

TAKE A POSITION OF PRAISE

When I was diagnosed with the inoperable brain tumor, there were 6 days between that initial diagnosis and the surgery to determine if it was a cancerous tumor. My husband, Mark, had spoken to the tumor to be dissolved in Jesus name. We did not spend those days begging and pleading, but in much praise and thanking God for His faithfulness and goodness.

Maybe you've prayed the prayer of faith, taken authority over the enemy, meditated on the scriptures concerning healing or paid your vows like Jonah did. The keys of thanking and praising God may be what you need to do now to open the door to your miracle. Open your heart, open your mouth and begin to reach out to receive whatever you need from God. His salvation, power and glory are as close as your heart and mouth (Romans 10:8-10).

MEDITATION POINT:
Because thy loving kindness is better than life, my lips shall praise thee. Thus will I bless thee while I live: I will lift up my hands in thy name. Psalm 63:3, 4

ACTION POINT:

_____

_____

_____

End Notes
1. *Noah Webster 1828 Dictionary,* http://1828.mshaffer.com
2. Strong, James, *The New Strong Exhaustive Concordance of the Bible,* H8426
3. Strong, James, T*he New Strong Exhaustive Concordance of the Bible,* G4982
4. Yeoman, Lillian, *Healing from Heaven*

Place By The Father

There is a place by the Father
And you can visit Him there
No darkness or fear can enter
But man in His glory can share

The secret place by the Father
His beauty you can behold
In Christ, the Rock of Ages
The story will ever be told

There is a place by the Father
At the right hand of His majesty on high
The place of His wonderful presence
And He welcomes you to draw nigh

- Mark Hankins

CHAPTER FOUR

Enter into Rest

One of my favorite things to do for my children and grand babies when they were infants was to put them to sleep. Sometimes there would be a period of time (seemed like hours) that I'd rock them or walk the floors with them when they would struggle, squirm and kick. They'd start to nod off, then suddenly open their sleepy eyes wide and begin to fuss. I'd go to patting and rocking, singing and bouncing until at last those eyes shut tight. If they were sucking a pacifier or their thumb, it would fall out of their mouth and I would feel their little arms stop fidgeting and they would completely relax. Then, it was time to tiptoe to the bed and gently lay them down for a good rest. This ritual wasn't finished until I leaned down for one more kiss on their soft cheek. Sometimes it would take a few minutes of watching carefully to make sure this was it, they're not going to wake up and fuss. There was nothing like seeing them sleeping in heavenly peace—mission accomplished.

This is the picture I see of the Heavenly Father who really cares for each of His children affectionately. Sometimes He sings songs of deliverance and peaceful assurance, whispering His faithful loving–kindness to us. We finally let go and enter into His rest. That is the place where it is done! No more struggle. Now there is a sweet release of every fear, anxiety or frustration. Hebrews 4:3 describes the rest of God as a place of complete trust in Him.

> *For we who have believed (adhered to and trusted in and rely on God) do enter that rest....*
>
> *Hebrews 4:3 (AMP)*

> *If we believe, though, we'll experience that state of resting....*
>
> *MSG*

TAKE HOLD ON GOD'S FAITHFULNESS

When I had asthma in the middle of the night, everyone was sleeping and I would try to be as quiet as I could while gasping for air. I'd get those scriptures out and make my eyes focus, drawing the life, hope and strength into my heart. If I could "look" with a steady, absorbing gaze like Numbers 21:9 in the Amplified Version says, the Word would seemingly come alive, jump off the page, enter my heart and my body would settle down, relax and I could breathe. What rest that followed!

There is a process of letting God's Word sink into your heart so much that you come to a resting place where you take hold of His faithfulness. In fact, Jesus told his listeners to let His sayings sink down into their ears (Luke 9:44). Imagine the Word of God sinking into your heart like an anchor plunging to the depths of the ocean and gripping the rock bottom. The thoughts of God lodge in the core of your being and you are convinced, settled on its reality and absolute truth.

Sarah received strength to conceive Isaac when she judged God faithful (Hebrews 11:11). The Amplified Bible says that "she considered [God] Who had given her the promise to be reliable and trustworthy and true to His Word." We need to get our gavel of faith out, affirm God's Word to be true and His character to be faithful. Like a judge, rest your case. God is faithful and true to you— now and forever! Now you have the faith of God (Mark 11:22). My favorite translation is the Century translation and it says, "Take hold on God's faithfulness."

ABOUNDING HOPE

May the God of your hope so fill you with all joy and peace in believing [through the

> *experience of your faith] that by the power*
> *of the Holy Spirit you may abound and be*
> *overflowing (bubbling over) with hope.*
>
> *Romans 15:13 (AMP)*

In the story of Abraham and Sarah, there came a time when Sarah was finished with trying to figure out how God would perform their miracle (having a son in their old age). She then entered into rest. That's when hope started bubbling up from the deepest part of her heart until it overflowed into a river of laughter that rejuvenated her very old body. What was that rest? It was the joy of the Lord. Like Sarah, when you enter into rest, you might find yourself smiling and laughing as you finally come face to face with God's faithfulness. You know He will perform His promise, but you've stopped trying to figure out how He will do it. You've entered into the rest of God.

> *For he who has once entered [God's] rest*
> *also has ceased from [the weariness and*
> *pain] of human labors, just as God rested*
> *from those labors...Let us therefore be zeal-*
> *ous and exert ourselves and strive diligent-*
> *ly to enter that rest [of God, to know and*
> *experience it for ourselves], that no one may*
> *fall or perish by the same kind of unbelief*
> *and disobedience [into which those in the*
> *wilderness fell]. For the Word that God*
> *speaks is alive and full of power [making it*

active, operative, energizing, and effective];
it is sharper than any two-edged sword,
penetrating to the dividing line of the breath
of life (soul) and [the immortal] spirit, and
of joints and marrow [of the deepest parts
of our nature], exposing and sifting and
analyzing and judging the very thoughts
and purposes of the heart.

Hebrews 4:10-12 (AMP)

My mother-in-law, Velma Hankins, used to say, "You are not trying the Word. No, the Word is trying you!" As you meditate on God's promises, saying them and seeing them, there may be a shaking of your thoughts and favorite traditions. The Word will try you and find the way of thinking which runs in your family and will actually put you in an early grave. However, you can embrace the Word as truth and the final authority and receive your healing.

JESUS IS PRAYING FOR YOU

My mother always reminds me of this empowering thought: Jesus Himself is praying to the Father God for us. He shares our feelings and gives us grace and well timed help coming just when we need it.

Inasmuch then as we have a great High
Priest Who has [already] ascended and
passed through the heavens, Jesus the Son

61

***of God, let us hold fast our confession [of
faith in Him]. For we do not have a High
Priest Who is unable to understand and
sympathize and have a shared feeling with
our weaknesses and infirmities and liability
to the assaults of temptation, but One Who
has been tempted in every respect as we are,
yet without sinning. Let us then fearlessly
and confidently and boldly draw near to the
throne of grace (the throne of God's unmer-
ited favor to us sinners), that we may receive
mercy [for our failures] and find grace to
help in good time for every need [appropri-
ate help and well-timed help, coming just
when we need it].***

Hebrews 4:14-16 (AMP)

When your body and a doctor's diagnosis are
screaming for your attention, it is time to turn your eyes to
Jesus alone. The way to do that is by looking at the Word
of God or listening to it being spoken or sung. Then, begin
to whisper, speak or sing a scripture to yourself, focusing
your entire attention on it.

I remember going into the MRI machine when I
was in the hospital. Instead of succumbing to claustro-
phobia, I got stronger because God sent a Word just in
time: "Surely when the great waters [of trial] overflow,
they shall not reach [the spirit] in him. You are a hiding
place for me; You, Lord, preserve me from trouble, You

surround me with songs and shouts of deliverance," Psalm 32:6, 7, AMP. The Spirit of God will take hold with you against your weakness. He is the Helper and I found that He is a very present help in the most difficult times.

Hebrews 3:1 calls Jesus the High Priest of our confession. That means He hears our confession and confirms it in Heaven before God the Father like an attorney would. This is a cooperation between you, God, and His Word. The Holy Spirit takes hold with you against your weakness with groanings too deep for words (Romans 8:26). When He hears your voice, He then confirms His Word with signs. The Holy Spirit gets down where you are and lifts you up. You run into the safety and strength of the arms of God.

David said in Psalm 18:6 that his cry went all the way to Heaven and to God's ears! That's when David said God had lit his candle or his spirit. He said, "For by You I can run through the troop; and by my God have I leaped over a wall. For you have armed me with strength for the battle," (Psalm 18:28-40).

JESUS, SAVE ME!

You may feel like Peter in Matthew 14 when he was walking on the water and began to sink. He got his eyes off Jesus and began to panic when he saw the waves all around him. The calm, strong voice of Jesus was lost in the shrieking sound of the wind. Panic overwhelmed him as the cold water and fierce waves threatened his life. He looked around, terror stricken and then screamed, "Jesus, save me!" Instantly, the strong grip of the Savior lifted him up to walk on top of the water again. Like Peter's cry, your cry is heard and help comes that only God can give! Listen to these words from Hebrews 6:18-20.

> *This was so that, by two unchangeable things [His promise and His oath] in which it is impossible for God ever to prove false or deceive us, we who have fled [to Him] for refuge might have mighty indwelling strength and strong encouragement to grasp and hold fast the hope appointed for us and set before [us]. [Now] we have this [hope] as a sure and steadfast anchor of the soul [it cannot slip and it cannot break down under whoever steps out upon it--a hope] that reaches farther and enters into [the very certainty of the Presence] within the veil, Where Jesus has entered in for us.*
>
> *Hebrews 6:18-20 (AMP)*

There is an anchor for your soul that reaches into the presence behind the veil. That means your mind, will and emotions are secured as you keep them fixed on God and His Word. Your hope is an expectation grounded on two things that cannot ever change: God's Word and His blood covenant. When Rahab, the harlot, knew the walls of Jericho were going to fall, her focus became the scarlet cord given to her by Joshua and Caleb. It represented their promise to Rahab that she, her family and possessions would be kept safe and sound. It was her hope. She had hope for her future. Everything might be falling around you, but keep your focus and expectation on the *scarlet cord* of God's Word and His covenant of Jesus' blood. They become the anchor for your soul that reaches into the very presence of God. This gives you peace that passes understanding, knowing that the answer is on the way.

FIND THE SECRET PLACE

He that dwelleth in the secret place of the most High shall abide under the shadow of the Almighty.

Psalm 91:1

When you believe there is a place you enter in
A place of peace and quiet rest
No more struggles, no more labors of your own
You've entered in the Rest of God

- Keith Moore [1]

One night while going through this collection of healing scriptures and fighting symptoms and pain, I came to the Knox translation of Psalm 91:3-4, "It is He that rescues me from every treacherous snare, from every whisper of harm. Sheltered under His arms, under His wings nestling, thou art safe: His faithfulness will throw a shield about thee."

As I read these scriptures, there was a lifting power and a peace that came alive on the inside. That is called a spoken word or *rhema* word from God. It is personal. I found that secret place and I knew I was abiding or dwelling in the Word and the Word was dwelling in me. In Jeremiah 49:30, God told Israel when they were under siege to "dwell deep." There is a place of quietness where there's no more struggle, but just resting or like the Knox translation expressed in Psalm 91:1, "He who lives under the protection of the Most High, under his heavenly care content to abide."

DWELL IN THE SECRET PLACE

And it shall come to pass, while my glory passeth by, that I will put thee in a cleft of the rock, and will COVER thee with my hand while I pass by.

Exodus 33:22

The word "cover" in this verse is *sakak* and means to entwine as a screen; by implication, to fence in, cover over, protect:--cover, defence, defend, hedge in, join together, set, shut up.[2] This covering is the place Moses found in the cleft of the rock as he saw God's glory go by. There is a place for us to abide where there is safety and healing. That place is in Christ where His body was broken and His side pierced so that anyone who puts faith in Him can enter in and find rest.

Enter in to this place in Christ and listen to His heart and His voice speaking to you. You can hear Him on the inside, especially after you've meditated on His Word or prayed in the Spirit. Then say what He says—it shall surely come to pass.

> *And the Lord will create over the whole site, over every dwelling place of Mount Zion and over her assemblies, a cloud and smoke by day and the shining of a flaming fire by night; for over all the glory shall be a canopy (a defense of divine love and protection). And there shall be a pavilion for shade in the daytime from the heat, and for a place of refuge and a shelter from storm and from rain.*
>
> *Isaiah 4:5-6 (AMP)*

God's covenant to you is one of divine love and protection. This is a place of refuge and shelter from the storms of sickness and disease. Take it for yourself as your covenant right and blessing.

Let me tell you about another particular time that I needed help. Like David described in Psalm 46:2, it seemed like the earth was being removed—now that is a bad day! I decided I needed some prayer help, so I called my "four faith-filled friends" to come into agreement with me. We presented this problem to the Father and began to yield to the Holy Spirit to give us help from the other side as Romans 8:26, 27 says He'll do. We prayed in the Spirit until there was a sense of breakthrough. What the enemy had designed for evil had been turned and stopped. The spirit of prophecy, which in the Hebrew means "to bubble up or flow like a fountain," and in the Greek means "to speak for God" came up from my heart. It released rivers of living water to stop the enemy. "When the enemy shall come in like a flood, the Spirit of the Lord will lift up a standard against him and put him to flight [for He will come like a rushing stream which the breath of the Lord drives]," Isaiah 59:19, AMP.

These are the words God gave to me at that moment and I continue to speak them daily and see wonderful results:

God is on my side
for the blood has been applied.
Every need shall be supplied
and nothing shall be denied.
So I enter into rest
and I know that I am blessed.
I have passed the test
and I will get God's best.

MEDITATION POINT:
If we believe, though, we'll experience that state of resting.
Hebrews 4:3 (MSG)

ACTION POINT:

_____

_____

_____

End Notes
1. Moore, Keith, *Rest of God*
2. Strong, James, The New Strong Exhaustive Concordance of the Bible, H5526

The Comfort of the Holy Spirit

The kind of comfort and consolation in distress which keeps a man on his feet, when left to himself, he would collapse. It is the comfort which enables a man or woman to pass the breaking point and not break. One who is called in to help in a situation with which a man by himself cannot cope. He (the Holy Spirit) exhorts men to high deeds and noble thoughts.

-William Barclay

CHAPTER FIVE

The Dynamic Power of Praying in the Spirit

The strong spirit of a man sustains him in bodily pain or trouble, but a weak and broken spirit who can raise up or bear?

Proverbs 18:14 (AMP)

The sounds in the hospital room were all around as I regained consciousness, but something much stronger was happening on the inside. Like a refreshing fountain of living water, healing scriptures were flowing up from my spirit and were much stronger than any pain I felt in my head.

The Holy Spirit has been sent to help us when we are weak and at the point of collapsing. He reminded me of this verse: *"In conclusion, be strong in the Lord [be empowered through your union with Him]; draw your strength from Him [that strength which His boundless might provides],"* Ephesians 6:10 (AMP). This scripture

71

stayed in my mind and held me steady throughout the entire ordeal. Being strong spiritually was the key to victory and that strength came from the power of the Holy Spirit.

This book would not be complete without giving testimony to the tremendous power of praying with the help of the Holy Spirit, or in other tongues. Many times I would have been overwhelmed and discouraged, but through this kind of prayer, I experienced exactly the help I needed at the moment. There are not only many spiritual benefits to this kind of prayer, but also physical ones discovered by those in the medical profession. In this chapter, we will focus on the physical and the spiritual advantages given to a Christian who exercises such a powerful prayer language.

THE HOLY SPIRIT, YOUR HELPER

Jesus introduced the person of the Holy Spirit before His death and resurrection, emphasizing how important it was to recognize and receive Him. The name Jesus used to describe the Holy Spirit is exactly what He does. The Holy Spirit is called the Comforter or Helper. The Greek word is *Paraclete* and the Amplified Bible in John 16:7 uses six words to describe what kind of help He can bring. They are: Counselor, Helper, Advocate, Strengthener, Intercessor and Standby.

Jesus introduced the Holy Spirit to His disciples like this:

However, I am telling you nothing but the truth when I say it is profitable (good, expedient, advantageous) for you that I go away. Because if I do not go away, the Comforter (Counselor, Helper, Advocate, Intercessor, Strengthener, Standby) will not come to you [into close fellowship with you]; but if I go away, I will send Him to you [to be in close fellowship with you].

John 16:7 (AMP)

William Barclay describes the work of the Holy Spirit or "Parakletos" this way:

The kind of comfort and consolation in distress which keeps a man on his feet, when left to himself, he would collapse. It is the comfort which enables a man or woman to pass the breaking point and not break. One who is called in to help in a situation with which a man by himself cannot cope. He exhorts men to high deeds and noble thoughts. [1]

Jesus told us to recognize the Holy Spirit and receive Him. Paul instructed us to yield to Him and to be led by Him. In the area of receiving healing, He is of utmost help. On the day of Pentecost in Acts 2, the Holy Spirit filled the new church with great power and they began to speak in languages unknown to them. People present from various nations understood what they were saying and heard them praising God. The results were great joy, miracles, boldness to witness about Jesus, and 3,000 people being saved. The promise was that this gift was for everyone and every generation (Acts 2:39).

If you study the use of speaking in tongues, which is unique to the New Testament church, you will discover that there are many benefits to this kind of spiritual expression. Let's examine the physical benefits of praying in tongues first. Medical science gives evidence to the physical benefits of this spiritual exercise.

THE PHYSICAL BENEFITS OF PRAYING IN TONGUES

A brain specialist was interested in finding out if there was a relationship between the brain and praying in tongues. He conducted research and several tests with some interesting results.

These are the physical benefits he found to praying in tongues. When we pray in tongues, we actively stimulate the hypothalamus, the part of our brain responsible for:

- the pituitary gland and all target endocrine glands
- the total immune system
- the entire autonomic system
- the production of brain hormones called endorphins and enkephalons, which are chemicals that the body

produces, and are <u>100 to 200 times more powerful</u> <u>than morphine</u>.

This means that when we pray in tongues, we are directly and indirectly stimulating a significant part of the body's central nervous system. This, in turn, causes the brain to release a large amount of hormones, increasing the body's immune system. Praying in tongues produces an effect similar to other physical activities like running and swimming. [2]

THE SPIRITUAL BENEFITS OF PRAYING IN TONGUES

A most interesting study was made by Dr. Andrew Newberg at the University of Pennsylvania. He wanted to see what happens in the brain during the deepest moments of faith. Senior Pastor Gerry Stoltzfoos of Freedom Valley Worship Center allowed the medical team to set up a brain scan on himself and a church member to observe the brain activity during praying in English and then, in "other tongues." The results were very clear. Prayers in English activated the frontal lobe of the brain while prayers prayed in "tongues" had no effect at all on the thinking part of the brain. This experiment was performed on Buddhist monks and Franciscan nuns. The difference was remarkable, revealing that during their meditation and prayers there was much brain activity. This scientifically supports the Bible truth that when a believer speaks in an unknown tongue, it is their spirit that is praying. Paul said in 1 Corinthians 14:14, "For if I pray in an unknown tongue, my spirit prays, but my understanding is unfruitful." [3]

Divine healing is a spiritual power from God and is received spiritually. Therefore, it is important to be spiritually strong to receive healing. Listed here are some of the spiritual benefits of praying in your spiritual language or what the scriptures call "other tongues." Since your faith is the determining factor in receiving spiritual blessing, you will see this kind of prayer powerfully strengthening your faith.

Speaking in tongues edifies or builds up your inner man on your faith.

- He who speaks in a tongue edifies himself. 1 Corinthians 14:4 (NKJV)
- But you, beloved, building yourselves up on your most holy faith, praying in the Holy Spirit. Jude 20 (NKJV)

Healing flows out of the rivers of living water in your spirit.

- He who believes in Me, as the Scripture has said, out of his heart will flow rivers of living water. John 7:38 (NKJV)
- And it shall be that every living thing that moves, wherever the rivers go, will live.... for they will be healed.... Ezekiel 47:9 (NKJV)

You receive power and boldness to speak the Word.

- But you shall receive power when the Holy Spirit has come upon you. Acts 1:8 (NKJV)
- And when they had prayed, the place where they were assembled together was shaken; and they were all filled with the Holy Spirit, and they spoke the word of God with boldness. Acts 4:31 (NKJV)

The Holy Spirit will take hold with you against your weakness.

- Likewise the Spirit also helps in our weaknesses. For we do not know what we should pray for as we ought, but the Spirit Himself makes intercession for us with groanings which cannot be uttered. Romans 8:26 (NKJV)

Praying in tongues releases the resurrection power of the Holy Spirit who gives life to your body.

- But if the Spirit of Him who raised Jesus from the dead dwells in you, He who raised Christ from the dead will also give life to your mortal bodies through His Spirit who dwells in you. Romans 8:11 (NKJV)

Your spirit is speaking directly to God while your mind is still.

- For he who speaks in a tongue does not speak to men but to God, for no one understands him; however, in the spirit he speaks mysteries. For if I pray in a tongue,

my spirit prays, but my understanding is unfruitful.
1 Corinthians 14:2, 14 (NKJV)

Speaking in tongues assists you in giving thanks to God.

• For you indeed give thanks well.
1 Corinthians 14:17 (NKJV)

The Holy Spirit fills you with God's love and helps you to stay in that love. You can release unhealthy emotions such as bitterness and anger, which can cause illness and hinder health.

• The love of God has been poured out in our hearts by the Holy Spirit. Romans 5:5 (NKJV)

• ...praying in the Holy Spirit, keep yourselves in the love of God.....Jude 20, 21 (NKJV)

The Holy Spirit quickens or makes alive the personal rhema word of God to you.

• It is the spirit that quickeneth...the words that I speak unto you, they are spirit, and they are life. John 6:63

• And take...the sword that the Spirit wields, which is the Word of God. Ephesians 6:17 (AMP)

Praying in the Spirit brings perfect rest.

• For with stammering lips and another tongue He will speak to this people, To whom He said, This is the rest with which You may cause the weary to rest, And, "This is the refreshing." Isaiah 28:11, 12 (NKJV)

You can unselfishly pray the perfect will of God concerning your physical situation.

* Now He who searches the hearts knows what the mind of the Spirit is, because He makes intercession for the saints according to the will of God. Romans 8:27 (NKJV)

Praying in the Spirit may not be easy at first, because your spirit is praying instead of your intellect. You may not be emotional or feel any special power or thrill. Don't be discouraged, but fortify yourself by being reminded of the spiritual benefits of praying in tongues.

The Holy Spirit will also help you to walk in love and forgive someone who has hurt or offended you. It is better to humble yourself and to confess your faults than to hold on to a grudge and die prematurely.

THE HOLY SPIRIT WILL GUIDE YOU

On many occasions David inquired of the Lord as to what to do. He needed a spirit of faith. There can be all kinds of voices and opinions about your case and it becomes very confusing. Well–meaning people give a variety of remedies and advice. That is a perfect time to seek the Lord by praying in tongues until your mind is quiet and your spirit is strong. Then meditate upon the healing scriptures and the voice of the Holy Spirit will speak clearly and decisively. He will help you to lay hold upon the rhema or spoken word of God. When you follow the promptings of the Holy Spirit, He will lead you to victory, just as He did for David. Your faith will be ignited by a word from God and by the Holy Spirit. Then you can run through the troop and leap over the wall!

One particular time, Mark and I had been traveling overseas and I came home sick. Then, one day I slipped and fell and had to get stitches in my hand. I went dragging in to the doctor and he advised me to stop traveling and stay home. That was not an option, because of our upcoming schedule of meetings. I was also trying to take care of our two young children so I felt very discouraged and overwhelmed. I looked to the Lord and spent time praying in other tongues. The mighty Holy Ghost sent this word right on time. These verses made all the difference for me then and even now, I find strength in them.

> *Do not rejoice over me, my enemy; When I fall, I will arise; When I sit in darkness, The Lord will be a light to me.*
> *Micah 7:8 (NKJV)*

> *For You will light my lamp; The Lord my God will enlighten my darkness. For by You I can run against a troop, By my God I can leap over a wall.*
> *Psalm 18:28, 29*

Being sensitive to the Holy Spirit as you meditate on the healing scriptures can make the difference between whether you experience healing or not. Jesus and the early church ministered healing to people in a variety of ways. Some had hands laid on them. Others received a command to get up and walk. One man even had mud put in his eyes and received his sight when he washed it off.

Others heard the Word, had faith to be healed, and rose up healed. Healing power can be received through the prayer of faith or when the sick one is anointed with oil in the name of the Lord (James 5:14–16). The Holy Spirit will always prompt you to act like the Bible is true and give you help in receiving healing.

> *The Holy Spirit will always prompt you to act like the Bible is true and give you help in receiving healing.*

THE HOLY SPIRIT WILL PROMPT YOU TO ACT IN FAITH

If you are in a play and you forget your lines, there is someone unseen by the audience, behind the curtains, who is there to help you when you need to speak. That person is called a prompter. The Holy Spirit is Heaven's prompter who has the script and knows what you need to say at the appointed time. Instead of being embarrassed and frozen in fear, listen to His promptings! Stop making up your own lines and begin speaking the words of the Author and Finisher of your faith. The Holy Spirit might prompt you to shout, laugh, praise, dance, rejoice, or even forgive somebody who offended you. If you have been praying in the language of the Spirit, you've got some assistance from the Comforter, Helper, Standby, Intercessor, Strengthener and Advocate.

Faith is an act. The moment you see or hear God's Word and it registers on your spirit, you need to act on the Word. Make an effort to move something and praise God, like the man Paul preached to at Lystra in Acts 14. When the man heard the gospel, Paul perceived he had faith to be healed and shouted at him, commanding him to rise in Jesus name. The man leaped and walked.

Don't wait or reason yourself out of a miracle. Yield to the Spirit of God and release your faith with an act. Praying in the Spirit will help you to receive what God has already done and made available to you. It releases the power of God. Like radiation, you may not feel a thing physically, but it is real and effectively working spiritually.

What kind of power does the Holy Spirit make available? Resurrection, hell–busting, disease destroying power! It is the same Spirit that anointed Jesus who went about doing good and healing all who were oppressed of the devil. It is the same Spirit that physically raised Christ from the dead. As you pray in the Spirit, His anointing will quicken your mortal body. When I meditated on the healing scriptures, I could see every cell and organ in my body being changed, made well and new. His Words are spirit and they are life. His power is spiritual power and though you may not feel anything, it will effect a healing and a cure, if you believe and act.

> *Don't reason yourself out of a miracle. Yield to the Holy Spirit and release your faith.*

WORSHIP IN THE SPIRIT

Let the rivers of healing flow out of your innermost being (John 7:38). I love this quote from Howard Carter, an evangelist who witnessed countless miracles of healing in his meetings in the early 1900's, about speaking with tongues.

> *We must not forget that praying in tongues is not only the initial evidence of the Holy Spirit's indwelling; it is the continual experience for the rest of one's life. For what purpose? To assist in the worship of God. Speaking in tongues is a flowing stream that should never dry up, for it will enrich a person's life spiritually.*
> *Howard Carter* [4]

INSPIRED WORSHIP RECEIVES MIRACLES

In Matthew 15, the Canaanite woman came to Jesus pleading with Him to deliver her daughter from demons. Because she was not a Jew, Jesus told her He wasn't sent to help her. The woman did something that changed everything and gave her access to the covenant that day. She fell down and worshiped Jesus and from that position, persisted in faith. "Even the dogs get the crumbs from master's table," she said. Jesus called that kind of faith "great" and her daughter was cured from that moment. Worshiping God opens your heart and at that point, anything is possible. Yield to the Spirit of God in worship to receive God's power.

The language of the Spirit is the language of Heaven where there is no sickness or pain. Through the precious blood of Jesus and the help of the Holy Spirit you can access the realm of life and health, drink from the rivers of life, and enjoy abundant life in the Spirit.

STRENGTH TO RECEIVE

Have you ever had a cell phone with little or no service because you are out of range of a satellite tower? You are talking along and all of a sudden you've dropped a call. Some locations have absolutely no connection and this can be a very frustrating thing. In efforts to get connected, you will pay any amount of money or even climb to a mountain top. How much more important is it to be spiritually connected. We have to have spiritual strength in order to transmit and receive the power of God for healing. Maybe you can't seem to grasp what the Word is saying, but if your spiritual muscles are strengthened, you can receive God's spiritual power and truth which will change your physical body.

There is a powerful prayer we can pray found in Ephesians 3:14-20, in which the Apostle Paul asks the Father God for spiritual strength. I pray this often and have found tremendous results when I have used it for myself and for others.

James 5:16 tells us the effectual, fervent prayer of a righteous man avails much. The Amplified version of that verse says it makes "tremendous power available, dynamic in its working." Spend time praying in tongues and experience greater strength working in you from the Greater One.

> *May He grant you out of the rich treasury of His glory to be strengthened and reinforced with mighty power in the inner man by the [Holy] Spirit [Himself indwelling your inner-most being and personality].*
> *Ephesians 3:16 (AMP)*

They laid hands on me
In the mighty Name of Jesus
His healing power went all through me
Bondage gave way to liberty

I'm reigning in life by Christ Jesus
His Word has set me free
The law of sin and death gave way
To the Spirit's law of Liberty

The power of healing is greater
Than the power of sickness and disease
His resurrection power is greater
And it's working in me now effectually

Julie Daniels

MEDITATION POINT:
May He grant you out of the rich treasury of His glory to be strengthened and reinforced with mighty power in the inner man by the [Holy] Spirit [Himself indwelling your innermost being and personality]. Ephesians 3:16 (AMP)

ACTION POINT:

_____
_____
_____

End Notes
1. Barclay, W, *New Testament Words*
2. Peterson, Dr. Carl, "Medical Facts about Speaking in Tongues"
3. Mabrey and Sherwood, "Speaking in Tongues: Alternative Voices in Faith"
4. Hagin, Kenneth, *Steps to Answered Prayer*

Keep thy heart with all diligence; for out of it are the issues of life.

- Proverbs 4:23

CHAPTER SIX

Hindrances to Receiving Your Healing

In the natural, some medicines don't work efficiently if taken improperly or combined with certain foods or other medications. The same is true about God's medicine. If your faith isn't working and results are not being seen, here are some areas that may need an adjustment.

1. IGNORANCE CONCERNING GOD'S WILL

The first hindrance to receiving healing is not knowing what the will of God is. His Word is His will and as you meditate on these scriptures you can be thoroughly convinced that it is His will to heal you. Some churches teach that the age of miracles have passed away. They say that God is trying to teach you something through your sickness. True, you may learn more about kindness, patience and dependence upon God, but a thorough study of the redemptive work of Jesus reveals clearly how sickness and disease came after Adam sinned and spiritual death entered. God was not only dealing with man's spiritual condition, but his physical condition. Jesus never turned away a sick person or told them to wait until they "learned a lesson" before they could be healed. If Jesus is the expression of God and He never changes (Hebrews 13:8), then we can be convinced of God's will concerning healing.

In Matthew 3, the leper came and asked Jesus if it was His will to heal. Jesus answered so clearly. I like the Basic English translation that reads, "It is my pleasure; be clean." The Knox translation states it simply, "It is my will." (See the section, *Healing is God's Will*)

2. UNPERSUADED TO ACT

Another hindrance to receiving the power of God in your life is being stubborn or unpersuaded to act on the Word of God. Mark 6:5, 6 tells us how Jesus could do no mighty works in His hometown because of their unbelief. Since faith and healing have a lot to do with your heart and are released by acting on what you know, it is vital to take the step to act on what you see in God's Word—to consider it the final authority. God has always and will always require us to act in faith in order to receive divine healing. The initial act of faith is to speak the Word of God (if you are physically unable to speak, use your method of commuication).

3. UNFORGIVENESS, BITTERNESS, STRIFE AND A WOUNDED SPIRIT

One of the major hindrances to your faith working is unforgiveness. Unforgiveness and bitterness are toxic and can lead to sicknesses such as heart disease, arthritis, cancer, ulcers, etc. Studies have been done in the medical field relating certain diseases to negative emotions. Some physical problems can be traced back to an event which opened the door for fear, strife, anxiety, anger or self pity. It is impossible to receive Heaven's power or for a person's faith to work if a person has not released an offense. Sometimes it is a small thing that stops the flow of healing, but it is deadly! This is what Jesus said to do:

> *When you stand praying, forgive, if you have ought against any: that your Father also which is in heaven may forgive your trespasses.*
>
> *Mark 11:25*

John Osteen told the Lord in a time of prayer, "Lord, I wish I could have heard one of your healing sermons." The Spirit of the Lord responded, "You can. My healing sermons are written in Matthew 5–7." If you study these chapters you will find the keys to health—spirit, soul, and body.

> *This is how I want you to conduct yourself in these matters. If you enter your place of*

91

worship and, about to make an offering, you suddenly remember a grudge a friend has against you, abandon your offering, leave immediately, go to this friend and make things right. Then and only then, come back and work things out with God.
Matthew 5:23, 24 (MSG)

In your prayer time, search your heart and ask the Holy Spirit to help you to see anything that would inhibit the healing power of God from working in your body. Sometimes we get comfortable with certain negative ways of thinking when actually it keeps our faith from working effectively.

One of the inhibitors to healing in my life was jealousy, which opened the door to anger. James 5:16 says to confess your faults one to another, and pray for one another, that you may be healed. I confessed this fault to my husband, he prayed for me and healing followed! At times things need to be confessed to the Lord, but also to someone spiritual who can pray for you to be healed.

The obstacle of bitterness and offense must be removed or it will continue to spread poison, not only through your own life but to those around you.

Jesus was teaching the disciples a lesson of faith and forgiveness when He used the example of the sycamore tree, which represents an offense (Luke 17:1-6). There are five facts about sycamore trees and we can learn valuable lessons from them.

1. The tree grows in dry places
2. The roots grow deep
3. The fruit is very bitter and is eaten by the poor
4. The wood is used for building coffins
5. It is pollinated by the stinger of a wasp

If you know how the enemy works, you won't fall into the trap of unforgiveness. Unforgiveness will cause you to live in a spiritually dry place, which is a dangerous place because Jesus said Satan goes around dry places finding an entrance into our lives (Matt. 12:43). Anger and unforgiveness can have deep roots. Like crabgrass takes over a lawn, anger and unforgiveness can take over your life. The roots of bitterness can also become widespread, affecting many others (Hebrews 12:15). Like the stinger of a wasp, the poison of bitterness is deadly. There may be deep roots of bitterness in your life, which can cause sickness and pain, but you have been given the authority and power to remove them.

Jesus said to speak TO the sycamore tree and cast it into the sea and it would obey you. With faith, the obstacles of offense can be dealt with. The sea can completely swallow any bitterness, hurt or offense so that you won't remember it.

FORGIVE YOURSELF

Sometimes the one you need to forgive is yourself. Instead of beating yourself up, just repent and receive forgiveness. "If we confess our sins He is faithful and just to forgive us our sins, and to cleanse us from all unrighteousness," 1 John 1:9. Hebrews 10:17 says God won't remember our sins because of the power of the blood of Jesus. He will cast them into the depths of the sea of mercy and they will be forgotten. *"He will turn again, he will have compassion upon us; he will subdue our iniquities; and thou wilt cast all their sins into the depths of the sea,"* Micah 7:19. It is done. No fishing allowed! God has forgotten them and so should you. The devil is called the accuser and you must overcome his accusations by the blood of the Lamb and the word of your testimony (Rev. 12:10, 11). My husband, Mark says, "If the blood of Jesus has the power to remove our sins from God's remembrance, it has the power to erase them from our minds."

> *If the blood of Jesus has the power to remove our sins from God's remembrance, it has the power to erase them from our minds.*

GUARD YOUR HEART

Keep thy heart with all diligence; for out of it are the issues of life.

Proverbs 4:23

Keep and guard your heart with all vigilance and above all that you guard, for out of it flow the springs of life.
                                    AMP

Keep vigilant watch over your heart; that's where life starts.
                                    MSG

There is a Old Testament promise given to everyone who would keep all the commandments and laws. The promise is that none of the diseases that came on others would come on them.

And said, If thou wilt diligently hearken to the voice of the Lord thy God, and wilt do that which is right in his sight, and wilt give ear to his commandments, and keep all his statutes, I will put none of these diseases upon thee, which I have brought upon the Egyptians: for I am the Lord that healeth thee.
                          Exodus 15:26

In the New Covenant there is a new commandment to love one another and there is a promise to those who walk in the God kind of love. *"So now I am giving you a new commandment: Love each other. Just as I have loved you, you should love each other,"* John 13:34, NLT. When we love and forgive others as He has loved and forgiven us, we are keeping the new commandment in the New Covenant and we have the same promise which God

95

gave Moses. None of these diseases shall come on you, because God is the Lord that heals you. You can claim this promise and resist satan and sickness. Say, "Devil, take your hands off my body! I am walking in love!" Sickness and disease is a curse of the law. Proverbs 26:2 says, "....the curse causeless shall not come." If we don't break God's laws, the curse cannot come and must leave when we obey the Word of God.

One of the commandments is to honor your father and mother so that you can live a long life (Eph. 6:1-3). I have a friend who was diagnosed with cancer. As he left the doctor's office after having received the report, he prayed, "Lord, I have not lived perfectly, but I have always honored my parents. The promise for doing that is long life, so I claim that promise now." He prayed and claimed that promise and cursed the cancer. The next time he was examined by the doctor, the cancer was gone and never came back. Honoring your parents is a part of the new commandment of walking in love. Many carry much bitterness from their childhood because of abuse from their parents or others and it shows up as various diseases. Thank God, He has made a way to be free.

4. *TURN YOUR FACE TO THE WALL*

There comes a time when you need to "turn your face to the wall," like Hezekiah did in 2 Kings 20. Not even the prophet's word to him that he was dying could shake him. This man's persistence laid hold on God and the prophet had to come back with a new word of healing for Hezekiah. Your faith can change the doctor's "prophecy" for your life expectancy! **Look to God alone!**

Dodie Osteen, sent home by the doctors to die of liver cancer, turned her face to the wall and took hold of God's power in the Word. Instead of going to bed, she kept doing everything a healed person would do. Instead of waiting until she felt healed to pray for others who were sick, she would force herself to get up, get to church and lay hands on the sick who came for healing. She had to almost crawl back to her seat at church, but she was keeping her faith active. Gradually, **the disease had to give way to the power of God.** A year later she was well and strong once more. Her strong spirit and faith in God, changed her body. [1]

5. FOUR "CRAZY" FRIENDS

Another key to having a breakthrough in the area of healing is having faith–filled relationships and going to a good church—a Spirit–filled church. A church where you hear the Word of God taught and there is freedom to praise God is vital to your life and health. I have gone to church many times with symptoms and before it was over, I was well. According to James 5:14,15 it is up to the one who is sick to call for prayer. When you ask for prayer, there is a release of your faith. Instead of staying home, get to where the healing praise, preaching, and the family of God are.

> *Everyone needs at least four crazy friends who believe with God all things are possible.*

In Luke 5:17-26 we read the story of four men who took their paralyzed friend to see Jesus. They came to the house where Jesus was teaching and couldn't get in, so they climbed to the roof, tore a hole in it and let their friend down right in front of Jesus. Jesus saw their faith and commanded the paralyzed man to rise and walk. My husband Mark says, "Everyone needs at least four crazy friends who believe with God all things are possible."

6. MAKE A COMMITMENT TO SERVE GOD

> *It is suggestive in James 5:15 that "The prayer of faith shall save the sick." The word translated means a vow. So that prayer in its highest form of faith is that prayer- which carries the whole man as a sacrificial offering.*
>
> *- E.M. Bounds* [2]

There are many examples in the Bible of great healing and deliverance coming after the person needing divine healing or deliverance prayed a prayer of commitment or paid their vows to God. For example, Hannah made a vow to give her child back to God to serve him. That is when her request for a child was granted. Jonah was released from the fish when he paid his vows to obey what God had told him to do. Dr. A.B. Simpson pointed out how he committed himself to God and made a vow to serve Him with his new found strength. Healing brings glory to God so we should continue to yield our healed bodies to serve Him.

> *Do you not know that your body is the temple of the Holy Spirit who is in you, whom you have from God, and you are not your own? For you were bought at a price; therefore glorify God in your body and in your spirit, which are God's.*
> *1 Corinthians 6:17-20 (NKJV)*

NOW - IT'S TIME TO ACT

As we meditate upon God's Word for healing, we will receive supernatural healing. Rejoice, praise, sing and laugh! This is how you release your faith. Say these scriptures to yourself. Think on what you are saying in your heart. Use them in praise to the Father. His Word is medicine to all your body. Let the Holy Spirit paint a picture on the canvas of your mind and heart of new cells, healed organs and healthy blood as you meditate on being redeemed from the curse of the law as Jesus hung on the cross.

> *It doesn't matter what the problem is, God's Word is just the medicine you need.*

Act on the Word by doing something you could not do before. Talk to your body and to symptoms with your God–given authority. It doesn't matter what the problem is, God's Word is just the medicine you need. When you receive your healing, don't forget to give thanks by living your life to glorify Jesus.

Dodie Osteen, who was healed from liver cancer by faith in God's Word, still makes time first thing every morning to meditate on her healing scriptures and to worship Jehovah Rapha, the One who healed her. Every day is a gift and opportunity to glorify God with our spirit, soul and body!

> **Bless the Lord, O my soul, and forget not all his benefits: Who forgiveth all thine iniquities; who healeth all thy diseases; Who redeemeth thy life from destruction; who crowneth thee with loving kindness and tender mercies; Who satisfieth thy mouth with good things; so that thy youth is renewed like the eagle's.**
>
> **Psalm 103:2-5**

Pray a prayer like this: *"Father, in Jesus Name, I release all offense I have held in my heart (you may be specific here). I confess my sin and I forgive anyone who has hurt me or wronged me. I release it and let it go. I speak to bitterness to be plucked out of my emotions and heart and cast into the midst of the sea, as Jesus said to do in Luke 17:6. Now I receive grace, mercy, life and healing. They are flowing like springs of living water from my spirit, bringing healing to my soul, which is my mind, will and emotions. The power of God is healing my body. I ask You, Father, to bless anyone who has hurt or wronged me in Jesus Name. You said you would heal me of all my wounds. I believe and receive healing now. Satan, I am free now from offense. Take your hands off me now! (Name your sickness or condition), I resist you and you must go. Thank you, Father, for healing me now. I know and believe it is Your will for me to be healed. Thank you, Jesus, for taking this sickness from me. Thank you, Holy Spirit, for your resurrection power working in my body now. I am healed. Ha! Ha! Ha! I rejoice! With joy I draw healing waters from the wells of salvation. A merry heart does good like a medicine."*

Oh, the glory is here
Yes, the glory is here
I can sense His mighty Presence
In the very atmosphere

For whatever you may need
Reach out and receive
And say, "Its mine!
I'll take it now"

Keith Moore [3]

MEDITATION POINT:

Keep and guard your heart with all vigilance and above all that you guard, for out of it flow the springs of life. Proverbs 4:23 (AMP)

ACTION POINT:

_____

_____

_____

End Notes
1. Osteen, Dodie, *Healed of Cancer*
2. Bounds, EM, *The Best of EM Bounds*
3. Moore, Keith, *The Glory is Here*

Live long–Live strong–
spirit, soul and body

May God himself, the God who makes everything holy and whole, make you holy and whole, put you together— spirit, soul, and body—and keep you fit for the coming of our Master, Jesus Christ.

- 1 Thessalonians 5:23 (MSG)

...may your spirit, soul, and body be kept healthy and faultless....

(CEV)

...may your spirit and soul and body be kept complete....

(LEB)

...may your spirit, soul, and body be kept intact...

(CEB)

CHAPTER SEVEN

Your Body is God's House

What? know ye not that your body is the temple of the Holy Ghost which is in you, which ye have of God, and ye are not your own? For ye are bought with a price: therefore glorify God in your body, and in your spirit, which are God's.

1 Corinthians 6:19-20

When you realize that you are God's dwelling place, it does two things: it makes you aware of the price He paid for your body and it makes you aware that you belong to God. It is His desire to live in you, so it's in God's best interest that you are strong physically. You bring glory to Him when you are healthy because He paid such a high price, the blood of Jesus, in order to purchase you—spirit, soul and body.

It also makes you aware that you have a responsibility to take care of your body properly. That means for you to exercise and eat nourishing foods.

If you purchase a computer, household appliance or vehicle, the first thing you usually do is to learn how it functions, the proper care and maintenance of it. There are regular tune-ups, oil changes and maintenance requirements for cars. You must use the proper gas and oil for the peak function of different kinds of engines. We do all these things for a machine, but we open our mouths and throw just about anything and everything in without giving it a second thought! Then we have to spend an enormous amount of money for operations and treatment of diseases that are a result of unhealthy lifestyles.

I like this little song I heard about healthy living:

Learn to relax, Get to bed on time
and do your exercise.
Breath fresh air while the sun's out there
and eat like this little rhyme.
Fruits and vegetables, whole grains.
White if you choose meat,
drink what you're mostly made of,
water will make your health complete. [1]

There are practical things we all can do in order to live out our years on the earth. They will cause us to be strong physically so we can do God's will and live life to the fullest, enjoying and being a blessing to those God puts in our path every day. Here are a few practical things we can do.

106

1. MOVE YOUR BODY

There are many great books, teachers and trainers which we can take advantage of in order to help us take care of our amazing temples of the living God. Physical exercise and stretching keep the bones and muscles strong, causing circulation and other systems to work efficiently. Paul told Timothy that bodily exercise profits for the little time that we're in our bodies. It is beneficial. It's better to have a good maintenance schedule than to have to fix broken down bodies. You bring glory to God with a healthy body.

If we exercise our pets and feed them proper food, how much more we should care about our bodies. We can maintain and see results as we practice a healthy lifestyle also.

2. WATER—THE DRINK OF CHOICE

Between 60-70 percent of your body is water; your brain is more than 80 percent water, your blood is more than 90 percent water. Dehydration creates a multitude of physical problems. It also gives illness and disease a chance to take hold. Many illnesses are exacerbated by or even result from chronic dehydration. Often when the doctor diagnoses an illness, you're not so much sick as you are thirsty. [2]

Many people live in a state of dehydration and don't know it. Sugar or caffeine–laden drinks make you thirstier and are also loaded with chemicals. Sometimes we think we're hungry when we are actually dehydrated and a good drink of water will energize and satisfy. Water cleanses away impurities inwardly and helps all our systems function properly. Just as you use water to rinse or flush away dirt, our bodies need cleansing in order to be free from infections and disease. We think more clearly and our joints move more easily when hydrated. Digestion and blood circulation work efficiently with the help of clear water. It is even the number one aid against facial complexion problems and signs of aging.

3. GET TO SLEEP

Our bodies need sleep! *Rest time is restoration time, and these days most of us have no idea what it's like to wake up feeling restored after a proper night's rest. I cannot over–emphasize the simple yet profound benefits of a good night's sleep....Actuarial figures from insurance companies show that people who go longer than seven days on five hours or fewer of sleep a night increase their risk of death from all causes by 700 percent! It has also been shown that people who sleep fewer than six hours a night don't live as long as people who sleep seven or more hours.* [3]

> **I laid me down and slept; I awaked; for the Lord sustained me.**
>
> **Psalm 3:5**

In peace I will both lie down and sleep, for You, Lord, alone make me dwell in safety and confident trust.

Psalm 4:8 (AMP)

He maketh me to lie down in green pastures: he leadeth me beside the still waters.

Psalm 23:2

When thou liest down, thou shalt not be afraid: yea, thou shalt lie down, and thy sleep shall be sweet.

Proverbs 3:24

It is vain for you to rise up early, to sit up late, to eat the bread of sorrows: for so he giveth his beloved sleep.

Psalm 127:2

Nothing thou shalt fear from nightly terrors.

Psalm 91:5 (Knox)

You will have no fear of the evil things of the the night.

Basic

4. SAY NO TO WORRY

One of the things keeping us awake is anxiety or stress. Anxiety, worry and the pressures of life are known causes of high blood pressure, digestion problems and heart disease. The Anglo-Saxon word for *anxiety* means "to strangle or choke." [4] Many things we worry about never happen and have to do with the natural things of life. Jesus addressed them in Matthew 6 as he taught about living differently from those who did not have a covenant relationship with God. Instead of worrying, we can pray, trust God and get busy seeking His kingdom first. Our Father in Heaven knows what we have need of.

> ***Do not fret or have any anxiety about anything, but in every circumstance and in everything, by prayer and petition (definite requests), with thanksgiving, continue to make your wants known to God. And God's peace [shall be yours, that tranquil state of a soul assured of its salvation through Christ, and so fearing nothing from God and being content with its earthly lot of whatever sort that is, that peace] which transcends all understanding shall garrison and mount guard over your hearts and minds in Christ Jesus.***
>
> ***Philippians 4:6, 7 (AMP)***

I'll never forget a lesson my dad taught me when I was about seventeen. He had been watching me worrying and stressing out about a decision I had to make. I was really working up a good anxiety attack. He stopped me and gave me these scriptures from Philippians 4. He said, "Trina, pray about that specific thing, thank God for helping you to make the right decision. Then lie down and go to sleep. In the morning when you wake up, the answer will come to you and you'll know exactly what to do." I remember doing what daddy said and just as he said, I had the answer before I opened my eyes!

ACTIONS WILL CHANGE YOUR EMOTIONS

If we will delight in Him, obey His instructions and pray about everything, His promise to us is that He will add everything we need to us (Matthew 6:33).

> *Thou will keep him in perfect peace, whose mind is stayed on thee: because he trusteth in thee.*
> *Isaiah 26:3*

> *And now, dear brothers and sisters, one final thing. Fix your thoughts on what is true, and honorable, and right, and pure, and lovely, and admirable. Think about things that are excellent and worthy of praise.*
> *Philippians 4:8 (NLT)*

> *We use our powerful God–tools for smashing warped philosophies, tearing down barriers erected against the truth of God, fitting every loose thought and emotion and impulse into the structure of life shaped by Christ.*
> *2 Corinthians 10:6 (MSG)*

We must guard our minds from wrong thinking, even if it comes from our family, church tradition or trends of the day!

111

Emotions have everything to do with good health. I highly recommend the book, *Deadly Emotions* by Dr. Don Colbert. In it, he discusses the direct correlation between negative emotions and the chemicals they release into the body which can lead to diseases. For example, anger can cause illnesses such as: tension headaches, migraine headaches, eczema, colitis, ulcers, asthma, hay fever, frequent urination and irritable bowel syndrome. It has been discovered that some back spasms result from tension, repressed anger, stress, frustrations and worry. Tension causes blood circulation to be constricted, causing a reduction of oxygen and blood supply to the tissues. The result is painful spasms and eventual numbness. Every negative emotion, such as fear, grief, depression, etc. can result in or be connected to various diseases or syndromes. (For further information, read *Deadly Emotions* by Dr. Don Colbert, M.D.) [5]

Again, the answer is found in the Word of God. Ephesians 4:26 says, ***"Be angry, and do not sin: do not let the sun go down on your wrath."*** I like the Johnson's paraphrase that puts it this way: "Admit your anger when you feel it, but don't be destructive with it. Learn insider ways of handling it properly." And Ephesians 4:31 in the Basic English Translation says, "Let all bitter, sharp and angry feeling, and noise, and evil words, be put away from you, with all unkind acts...." The next verse is a key to vital health because it deals with having a tender heart, which is the part of you from which healing and life flow. "And be ye kind one to another, tender hearted, forgiving one another, even as God for Christ's sake hath forgiven you."

Physical health is intertwined with the state of our minds and spirits. That's why meditating on these healing scriptures until they are part of you will tear down any thought that is not in agreement with God's Word and in it's place, establish the truth. What happens when you know the truth? Freedom! *"If you abide in My word, you are My disciples indeed. And you shall know the truth, and the truth shall make you free,"* John 8:31-32 (NKJV).

I have an aunt who has been healed of bone cancer through the power of the Word of God and prayer. I remember giving her a scripture over the telephone. At that time, she was skin and bones and the doctors did not give her any hope. She wrote that verse down immediately and began to meditate on it and declare it as truth about her own body. That's how she treated each scripture that came to her—like a treasure. She defied what the medical profession said about her. Today she is a picture of health and a sign and wonder to her doctors. Instead of worrying and seeing herself dying, she laughed frequently, prayed about everything, and lived anxiety free through prayer and praise.

> **Beloved, I pray that you may prosper in all things and be in health, just as your soul prospers.**
>
> *3 John 2*

5. LAUGHTER - DOES GOOD LIKE A MEDICINE

Laughter, the best medicine, has been proven to have great and amazing affects on the human body. For example, Parkinson's disease is caused by a deficiency in dopamine and it is said that there's no way to administer it to the human body except through laughter. It even has a positive effect on the liver. Hormones called endorphins are natural pain killers released by laughter. A merry heart <u>does</u> good like a medicine!

According to Dr. Gjerdingen, a family physician and professor at the University of Minnesota Medical School, humor promotes good health.

Humor is defined as a stimulus that helps people laugh and feel happy, while laughter is a response to humor that involves positive physiological and psychological reactions. The positive emotions associated with laughter and humor involve the dopamine system of the brain. When one laughs, various muscle groups are activated, but the period after the laugh is characterized by general muscle relaxation, which can last up to 45 minutes. Greater relaxation is seen with true laughter, compared to simulated laughter. [6]

Melissa Breyer, an author for "Healthy Living," shows what happens physiologically and psychologically when a person laughs. Here are just a few things it does:

- **Lowers blood pressure**
- **Increases vascular blood flow and oxygenation of the blood**
- **Gives a workout to the diaphragm and abdominal, respiratory, facial, leg, and back muscles**
- **Reduces certain stress hormones such as cortisol and adrenaline**
- **Increases the response of tumor and disease–killing cells such as Gamma–interferon and T–cells**
- **Defends against respiratory infections (even reducing the frequency of colds) by immuno-globulin in saliva**
- **Increases memory and learning (in a study at Johns Hopkins University Medical School, humor during instruction led to increased test scores)**
- **Improves alertness, creativity, and memory** [7]

You see the benefits of laughter. How much more the joy of the Lord can do to bring health and healing. Go ahead, draw up healing power out of your spirit with a deep belly laugh!

6. SHOULD I SEE A DOCTOR?

It is not a sign of weakness to make a doctor appointment if you are having symptoms in your body

115

or are suffering physically. I had a friend who refused to go to the doctor when she had alarming symptoms in her body. She said all the right things but she would never seek medical attention because she was afraid of the doctor's report. God has not given us a spirit of fear (2 Tim. 1:7). She had mental assent, but not Bible faith. This young wife and mother went to Heaven, but her life was taken prematurely. Don't mistake belief for healing with the God kind of faith. Jesus said to fear not; only believe. You can visit your doctor and be in faith at the same time.

Jesus said to speak to the mountain and sometimes you need to know what the mountain is so you can target your faith. Trust the Great Physican to be your Chief Physican. He will guide you to the best doctor so you can receive the right treatment for your situation. We are not working against the medical profession but God can work supernaturally through the medicine.

If you have an operation or take medication, it doesn't mean you don't have faith. Continue to meditate on the Word as your faith grows to another level and you will live a long life full of health and strength.

MEDITATION POINT:
A cheerful heart is good medicine, but a broken spirit saps a person's strength. Proverbs 17:22 (NLT)

ACTION POINT:

_____

_____

_____

End Notes
1. Verhulst, Dr. Don, *10 Keys that Cure*
2. Verhulst, Dr. Don, *10 Keys that Cure*
3. Verhulst, Dr. Don, *10 Keys that Cure*
4. Anglo-Saxon
5. Colbert, Dr. Don, *Deadly Emotions*
6. Gjerdingen, Dr. Dwenda, *The Network A Called Community of Women*
7. Breyer, M. *Care2Make a Difference*

Go up into Gilead and take
[healing] balm...

- Jeremiah 46:11 (AMP)

SECTION TWO:

God's Prescription
for Healing

Healing Scriptures and Confessions

FOR HEALING

DIRECTIONS: Read each scripture. If one stands out to you, mark it. Confession means to say the same thing. That means you put the scriptures in your own words and say them out loud, thinking about what you are saying. If you are physically unable to speak, use your method of communication.

PRESCRIPTION: Take daily as frequently as desired with deep drinks of living water from the River of Life. Results are increased if you smile or laugh out loud.

1. *MAKE A CHOICE TO RECEIVE HEALING*

I call heaven and earth as witnesses today against you, that I have set before you life and death, blessing and cursing; therefore choose life, that both you and your descendants may live.

Deuteronomy 30:19 (NKJV)

2. *USE YOUR VOICE*

Death and life are in the power of the tongue, And those who love it will eat its fruit.

Proverbs 18:21 (NKJV)

3. *THINK, ACT AND SPEAK GOD'S WORD ONLY*

But He answered and said, "It is written, 'Man shall not live by bread alone, but by every word that proceeds from the mouth of God.'"

Matthew 4:4 (NKJV)

Don't fool yourself into thinking that you are a listener when you are anything but, letting the Word go in one ear and out the other. Act on what you hear! Those who hear and don't act are like those who glance in the mirror, walk away, and two minutes later have no idea who they are, what they look like.

James 1:22-24 (MSG)

My son, give attention to my words; Incline your ear to my sayings. Do not let them depart from your eyes; Keep them in the midst of your heart; For they are life to those who find them, And health to all their flesh.

Proverbs 4:20-22 (NKJV)

Then the Lord said to me, "You have seen well, for I am ready to perform My word."

Jeremiah 1:12 (NKJV)

For He Himself has said, "I will never leave you nor forsake you." So we may boldly say: "The Lord is my helper; I will not fear. What can man do to me?"

Hebrews 13:5, 6 (NKJV)

4. DEPEND ON THE HOLY SPIRIT TO HELP YOU

[Not in your own strength] for it is God Who is all the while effectually at work in you [energizing and creating in you the power and desire], both to will and to work for His good pleasure and satisfaction and delight.

Philippians 2:13 (AMP)

*...I am the Lord
that healeth thee.*
- Exodus 15:26

CHAPTER EIGHT

Healing is God's Will

EXODUS 15:25, 26 And he cried unto the Lord; and the Lord shewed him a tree, which when he had cast into the waters, the waters were made sweet: there he made for them a statute and an ordinance, and there he proved them, and said, If thou wilt diligently hearken to the voice of the Lord thy God, and wilt do that which is right in his sight, and wilt give ear to his commandments, and keep all his statutes, I will put none of these diseases upon thee, which I have brought upon the Egyptians: for **I am the Lord that healeth thee.**

(NEW ENGLISH BIBLE) …I, the Lord, am your healer.

(LEESER)… for I, the Lord, am thy physician.

(BASIC) …I am the Lord your life-giver.

(ROTH) …I am Yahweh, thy physician.

(YOUNG) …I, Jehovah, am healing thee.

(SMITH-GOODSPEED) …for I, the Lord, make you immune to them (diseases).

(KNOX) …I, the Lord, will bring thee only health.

CONFESSION: God is speaking to me now, saying, "I am the Lord that healeth thee." He is watching over His Word to perform it. He is the Lord that healeth me. He is healing me now. This Word contains the ability to produce what it says. He is the Lord that healeth me. His Word is full of healing power now. Healing is in God's nature. God is in me. My body is the temple of God. My body is the temple of the Lord that healeth me. God is bigger than sickness and Satan. God is dwelling inside of me now, healing me now. The Lord that healeth me is my Shepherd; I do not lack healing. My body is in contact with the Lord that healeth me. My body has to respond to God's healing life and nature at work in me now. Healing is in God and God is in me. "I thank you, Father, because you are my Healer and You are healing me now."

EXODUS 23:25 And ye shall serve the Lord your God, and he shall bless thy bread, and thy water; and I will take sickness away from the midst of thee.

(BASIC) And give worship to the Lord your God, who will send his blessing on your bread and on your water; and I will take all disease away from among you.

(MOF, SMITH-GOODSPEED) …I will free you from disease.

(YOUNG) …I have turned aside sickness from thine heart.

(KNOX) …and keep sickness away from thy company.

CONFESSION: "I will" is the strongest assertion that can be made in the English language. God is speaking to me now saying, "I will take sickness away from the midst of thee." God is watching over His Word, performing it in me now. He is taking sickness away from the midst of me. I worship the Lord my God who takes sickness away from the midst of me. Goodbye, sickness; the Lord is taking you away from the midst of me. Thank you, Father, for taking sickness away from me. I thank you for doing what you said.

DEUTERONOMY 7:15 And the Lord will take away from thee all sickness, and will put none of the evil diseases of Egypt, which thou knowest, upon thee...

CONFESSION: The Lord is taking away from me all sickness. His Word contains the ability to do what it says. His Word will not return void but accomplish what it was sent to do. The Lord is taking away from me all sickness, every trace of weakness and deficiency. Sickness is going out of me now. Thank you, Father, for taking away from me all sickness like you said you would.

JEREMIAH 30:17 For I will restore health unto thee, and I will heal thee of thy wounds, saith the Lord; because they called thee an Outcast.

127

(KNOX) Then I will heal that scar of thine, the Lord says, cure thee of thy wounds;

(NLT) "I will give you back your health and heal your wounds," says the Lord.

(AMP) For I will restore health to you, and I will heal your wounds, says the Lord.

(S.R. DRIVER) For I will bring up fresh flesh for thee, and I will heal you of your wounds, saith Yahweh.

(MSG) As for you, I'll come with healing, curing the incurable, because they all gave up on you and dismissed you as hopeless.

CONFESSION: God has declared that He would restore my health and heal me of every wound. I receive complete restoration, fresh flesh and vitality. There is nothing hopeless, for God has given me His Word that He would heal and cure the incurable. When others give up hope, I put my hope in God who gives me fresh flesh and complete healing!

JEREMIAH 32:27 Behold, I am the Lord, the God of all flesh: is there any thing too hard for me?

(KNOX) Am I not the Lord, the God of all that lives? How should any task be too difficult for me?

CONFESSION: God, I take you at your Word that nothing is too hard for you! You are the same God who has healed every disease, sickness and condition. You

are the same yesterday, today and forever and I turn my eyes only to you now. I praise and magnify your ability now!

MATTHEW 8:2,3 And, behold, there came a leper and worshipped him, saying, Lord, if thou wilt, thou canst make me clean. And Jesus put forth his hand, and touched him, saying, I will; be thou clean. And immediately his leprosy was cleansed.

(JER) A leper now came up and bowed low in front of him. "Sir," he said, "if you want to, you can cure me." Jesus stretched out His hand, touched him and said, "Of course I want to! Be cured!" And his leprosy was cured at once.

(WADE) …if you have the will, you have the power to cleanse me….I have the will; be cleansed.

(JORDAN) …Sir, if you really wanted to, you could heal me. …I do want to.

(PHILLIPS) …if you want to, you can make me clean… Of course I want to. Be clean!

(BASIC) …Lord, if it is your pleasure, you have the power to make me clean. And He put His hand on him, saying, It is my pleasure; be clean.

(RIEU) …I will it. Be cleansed.

(KNOX) …It is my will…

(FENTON, WEYM, 20TH CR) I am willing…

(WUEST) …I am desiring it from all my heart. Be cleansed at once.

(AUTHENTIC) …I do will it…

CONFESSION: God wants me well. Healing is the will of God. God is at work in me right now to will and to do His good pleasure (Philippians 2:13). Healing is at work in me. It brings God pleasure for me to be healed.

MATTHEW 9:34, 35 But the Pharisees said, He casteth out devils through the prince of the devils. And Jesus went about all the cities and villages, teaching in their synagogues, and preaching the gospel of the kingdom, and healing every sickness and every disease among the people.

(TLB) …And wherever he went he healed people of every sort of illness.

(AMP) But the Pharisees said, He drives out demons through and with the help of the prince of demons. And Jesus went about all the cities and villages, teaching in their synagogues and proclaiming the good news (the Gospel) of the kingdom and curing all kinds of disease and every weakness and infirmity.

(NIV) …preaching the good news of the kingdom and healing every disease and sickness.

(BASIC) …making well all sorts of disease and pain.

(GSPD) ...proclaiming the good news of the kingdom, and curing every disease and illness.

(ASV) ...healing all manner of disease and all manner of sickness.

CONFESSION: Jesus is the same yesterday, today and forever. If He healed every sickness, disease and pain 2,000 years ago, His will is the same today. I receive the teaching of Jesus today. It is the thief who comes to steal, kill and to destroy, but Jesus came to give me abundant life (John 10:10). I see that the kingdom of God includes healing. I believe the good news.

HEBREWS 13:8 Jesus Christ the same yesterday, and to day, and for ever.

(AMP) Jesus Christ (the Messiah) is [always] the same, yesterday, today, [yes] and forever (to the ages).

(KNOX) What Jesus Christ was yesterday, and is today, he remains forever.

(MOF) Jesus Christ is always the same....

CONFESSION: I believe Jesus always healed all sickness and disease. He never turned anyone away. If He is the same yesterday, today and forever, I know it is God's will to heal me now.

PSALM 30:2 O Lord my God, I cried unto thee, and thou hast healed me.

CONFESSION: I believe I have received my healing (Mark 11:24). You have healed me. I don't consider

what I feel. I believe I am healed. Thou hast healed me.

PSALM 42:11 Why art thou cast down, O my soul? and why art thou disquieted within me? hope thou in God: for I shall yet praise Him, who is the health of my countenance, and my God.

(AMP) Why are you cast down, O my inner self? And why should you moan over me and be disquieted within me? Hope in God and wait expectantly for Him, for I shall yet praise Him, Who is the help of my countenance, and my God.

CONFESSION: I refuse to be cast down or discouraged. I am the conqueror. I will yet praise Him, who is the health of my countenance and my God. Father, I praise you because You are the health of my countenance.

PROVERBS 18:14 The spirit of a man will sustain his infirmity; but a wounded spirit who can bear?

(MSG) A healthy spirit conquers adversity, but what can you do when the spirit is crushed?

(ISR98) The spirit of a man sustains him in sickness

(GNT) Your will to live can sustain you when you are sick, but if you lose it, your last hope is gone.

CONFESSION: I am strong in the Lord and in the power of His might. I am strengthened with power by

His Spirit in my inner man. Therefore, with my spirit that is in union with Christ, I can conquer sickness in my body. I will overcome because my hope is steadfast in Christ, who is my Rock.

PSALM 91:1-6, 10 1 He that dwelleth in the secret place of the most High shall abide under the shadow of the Almighty. 2 I will say of the Lord, He is my refuge and my fortress: my God; in Him will I trust. 3 Surely he shall deliver thee from the snare of the fowler, and from the noisome pestilence. 4 He shall cover thee with his feathers, and under his wings shalt thou trust: his truth shall be thy shield and buckler. 5 Thou shalt not be afraid for the terror by night; nor for the arrow that flieth by day; 6 Nor for the pestilence that walketh in darkness; nor for the destruction what wasteth at noonday. 10 There shall no evil befall thee, neither shall any plague come nigh thy dwelling.

(AMP) [1]He who dwells in the secret place of the Most High shall remain stable and fixed under the shadow of the Almighty [Whose power no foe can withstand].

(LEESER) [1]He who sitteth under the secret protection of the Most High, shall rest under the shadow of the Almighty.

(NEW WORLD) [1]Anyone dwelling in the secret place of the Most High will procure himself lodging under the very shadow of the Almighty One.

133

(**BYINGTON**) [1]One who lives under the Most High's screen, lodges under Shaddai's canopy.

(**RSV**) [1]He who dwells in the shelter of the Most High, who abides in the shadow of the Almighty, [2]will say to the Lord, "My refuge and my fortress; my God, in whom I trust."

(**YOUNG**) [1]He who is dwelling in the secret place of the Most High, in the shade of the Mighty lodgeth habitually, [2]He is saying of Jehovah....

(**SMITH-GOODSPEED**) [1]He who dwells...[2]Says of the Lord....

(**KNOX**) [1]He who lives under the protection of the Most High, under his heavenly care content to abide, [2]can say to the Lord, Thou art my support and my strong hold, my God in whom I trust. [3]It is He that rescues me from every treacherous snare, from every whisper of harm. [4]Sheltered under his arms, under his wings nestling, thou art safe; his faithfulness will throw a shield about thee.

(**BASIC**) [1]Happy is he whose resting-place is in the secret of the Lord, and under the shade of the wings of the Most High; [2]Who says of the Lord, He is my safe place and my tower of strength: he is my God...[3] He will take you out of the bird-net, and keep you safe from wasting diseases.

(**GOOD NEWS**) [3]He will keep you safe from all hidden dangers and from all deadly disease.

(**BECK**) [3]...and from the deadly plague.

(LIVING BIBLE) [4]...His faithful promises are your armor.

(KNOX) [5]Nothing thou shalt fear from nightly terrors... [6] from the assault of man or fiend under the noon.

(BASIC) [5] You will have no fear of the evil things of the night...[6] Or of the disease which takes men in the dark....

(BECK) [6]...the plague ravaging at noon.

(NAB) [6]...nor the devastating plague at noon.

(NIV) [6]...nor the plague that destroys at midday.

(LEESER) [6]...nor of the deadly disease that wasteth at noonday.

(NEW WORLD) [9]Because you [said]: "Jehovah is my refuge," You have made the Most High Himself your dwelling.

(BASIC) [9]Because you have said, I am in the hands of the Lord, the Most High is my safe resting- place.

(NEB) [10] No disaster will befall you, no calamity shall come upon your home.

(KNOX) [10]There is no harm that can befall thee....

(SMITH-GOODSPEED) [10]No disaster will befall you, nor calamity come near your tent.

(GOOD NEWS) [10] And so no disaster will strike you, no violence will come near your home.

(FENTON) [10] So sickness will not approach you, contagion not enter your Rest.

CONFESSION: I'm abiding under the shadow of the Almighty. Jehovah-Rapha, the Lord that healeth me, is my refuge and fortress against disease. His Word is my shield and buckler against sickness. I'm trusting under His wings, and there is healing in His wings (Malachi 4:2). I'm not afraid of disease. I am not afraid of sickness. I'm abiding under the shadow of Jehovah-Rapha, the Lord that healeth me. No plague shall come nigh my dwelling or my body.

3 JOHN 2 Beloved, I wish above all things that thou mayest prosper and be in health, even as thy soul prospereth.

(BASIC) My loved one, it is my prayer that you may do well in all things, and be healthy in body, even as your soul does well.

(FENTON) I pray above all, friend, that you may be prosperous and well, just as your soul prospers.

(BARCLAY) My dear friend, it is my prayer that everything is going well with you, and that you are in good health.

(MSG) We're the best of friends, and I pray for good fortune in everything you do, and for your good health—that your everyday affairs prosper, as well as your soul!

(NLT) Dear friend, I hope all is well with you and that you are as healthy in body as you are strong in spirit.

CONFESSION: I am prospering and I am in health,

even as my soul prospers, because it is God's will for me. God is at work in me to will and to do His pleasure. Jehovah-Rapha is at work in me, healing me. He is the Lord that healeth me. God is greater than the devil. Healing is greater than sickness. God is at work in me, healing me.

JOHN 10:10 The thief cometh not, but for to steal, and to kill, and to destroy: I am come that they might have life, and that they might have it more abundantly.

(CEB) ....I came so that they could have life—indeed, so that they could live life to the fullest.

(MSG)....I came so they can have real and eternal life, more and better life than they ever dreamed of.

(NLT) ....The thief's purpose is to steal and kill and destroy. My purpose is to give life in all its fullness.

CONFESSION: Jesus is the expression of the Father God. Jesus carried out God's will and purpose in the earth. He wants me to live life to the fullest, to enjoy a rich and satisfying life, and have a better life than I can dream of. The devil, the thief, is the one who has tried to steal my health, to kill and to destroy my life. I choose now to receive the life of Christ, the Healer. The thief cannot destroy my life now because I am convinced that God's will for me is a healthy, abundant life.

He sent his word, and healed them, and delivered them from their destructions.

- Psalm 107:20

CHAPTER NINE

Healing through God's Word

PSALM 107:20 He sent his word, and healed them, and delivered them from their destructions.

(MOF) He sent his Word to heal them and preserve their life.

(LEESER) …and delivereth them from their graves.

(FENTON) He sent out His word, and it healed, and from their corruptions it freed.

(AMP) He sends forth His word and heals them and rescues them from the pit and destruction.

(MSG) He spoke the word that healed you, that pulled you back from the brink of death.

CONFESSION: He sent His Word and healed me. His Word heals me and delivers me from my destructions. His Word frees me from my corruptions. God's Word contains God's ability to perform what it says (Isaiah

139

55:10, 11). His Word is healing me now. His Word contains His healing power. His Word is working in me now. He has sent His Word and healed me and rescued me, pulling me back from the brink of death! Thank you, my God, for sending your Word.

PROVERBS 4:20-22 My son, attend to my words; incline thine ear unto my sayings. Let them not depart from thine eyes, keep them in the midst of thine heart. For they are life unto those that find them, and health to all their flesh.

(LIVING BIBLE) …let them penetrate deep within your heart.

(KNOX) Let a man master them, they will bring life and healing to his whole being.

(LEESER) …and to all his body a healing.

(ROTH) …to every part of one's flesh they bring healing.

CONFESSION: God's Word is health to all my flesh. His Word is medicine to my flesh. "I am the Lord that healeth thee," is medicine to my flesh now. "I will take away from thee all sickness," is medicine to all my flesh. The Word of God is full of the life of God. That life is saturating my spirit. God's life and healing power are in His Word and His Word is at work in me now. The Word of God is depositing the life of God and the healing of God into my spirit. That life and health are

spreading out of my spirit into every tissue and pore of my body, creating health and soundness. My body has no choice but to respond to the healing in the Word that is being absorbed into me now.

PROVERBS 12:18 There is that speaketh like the piercings of a sword: but the tongue of the wise is health.

(MOF) A reckless tongue wounds like a sword, but there is healing power in thoughtful words.

(GOOD NEWS) Thoughtless words can wound as deeply as any sword, but wisely spoken words can heal.

(BASIC) There are some whose uncontrolled talk is like the wounds of a sword, but the tongue of the wise makes one well again.

CONFESSION: My tongue makes me well. I have what I say. I say, "The Lord is my Healer." I say, "He takes sickness away from me." I say, "No plague comes nigh my dwelling." I will say, "He heals all my diseases." What I confess, I possess. My words make me well. There is healing power in my words, for they are God's words. I speak health to every muscle, tissue, fiber and cell in my body. I release God's healing power with my words into my whole body. Healing is mine.

MARK 5:25-34 And a certain woman, which had an issue of blood twelve years, And had suffered many things of many physicians, and had spent all that she had, and was nothing bettered, but rather grew worse, When she had heard of Jesus, came in the press behind, and touched his garment. For she said, If I may touch but his clothes, I shall be whole. And straightway the fountain of her blood was dried up; and she felt in her body that she was healed of that plague. And Jesus, immediately knowing in himself that virtue had gone out of him, turned him about in the press, and said, Who touched my clothes? And his disciples said unto him, Thou seest the multitude thronging thee, and sayest thou, Who touched me? And he looked round about to see her that had done this thing. But the woman fearing and trembling, knowing what was done in her, came and fell down before him, and told him all the truth. And he said unto her Daughter, thy faith hath made thee whole; go in peace, and be whole of thy plague.

(WILLIAMS) ...for she kept saying; If I can only touch his clothes, I shall get well.

(WUEST) ...for she kept saying, If I touch even His garments, I shall be made whole.

(PHILLIPS) ...she kept saying....

(AUTHENTIC) Jesus also was immediately aware that power had been drawn from Him....

(WADE) ...Jesus, becoming conscious that the healing power within Him had been in active operation....

(SMITH-GOODSPEED) Jesus instantly perceived that healing power had passed from him....

142

(20TH CR) Jesus instantly became conscious that there had been a demand upon his powers…your own faith has made you well….

(BARCLAY) …Go and enjoy your new health, free from the trouble that was your scourge.

(DIAGLOTT) …be entirely free from thy disease.

(AMP) …Go in (into) peace and be continually healed and freed from your [distressing bodily] disease.

CONFESSION: Her faith made her whole and my faith makes me whole. I have faith, for I am a believer. I believe I receive my healing, and my faith makes me whole. The power that raised Christ from the dead is at work in me (Ephesians 1:19). My faith puts that power into active operation in my body. Disease has no chance for survival in my body. The power that raised Jesus from the dead is at work in me. That power is irresistible; it is greater than sickness and disease. That power is flowing in me and makes me whole. I believe I have received my healing, and my faith has made me whole.

Blessed Redeemer

Blessed Redeemer,
Bore my sickness and my pain
Now I don't ever have to bear them
Oh, praise Your Name

Blessed Redeemer,
Suffered agony and shame
So I could live in health and happiness
Oh, praise Your Name

Though the devil screams and shouts
That cannot be
I will never cease to say
He has healed me

Blessed Redeemer
Without a doubt You bore it all
There's not one thing that You've forgotten
You're my all in all

-Keith Moore

CHAPTER TEN

Redeemed from the Curse of Sickness

ISAIAH 53:3-5 He is despised and rejected of men; a man of sorrows, and acquainted with grief: and we hid as it were our faces from him; he was despised, and we esteemed him not. Surely he hath borne our griefs, and carried our sorrows: yet we did esteem him stricken, smitten of God, and afflicted. But he was wounded for our transgressions, he was bruised for our iniquities: the chastisement of our peace was upon him; and with his stripes we are healed.

> These are notes concerning Isaiah 53:3–5 from the book *Christ The Healer.* The author, F.F. Bosworth, a powerful minister who saw countless people healed as he taught and ministered healing in the early 1900's.

145

In the fourth verse, the word borne (nasa) means " to lift up, to bear away, to convey or to remove to a distance." It is a Levitical word and is applied to the scapegoat that bore away the sins of the people. "The goat shall bear [nasa] upon him all their iniquities unto a land not inhabited: and he shall let go the goat into the wilderness" (Leviticus 16:22). So Jesus bore my sins and sicknesses away "without the camp"to the cross. Sin and sickness have passed from me to Calvary—salvation and health have passed from Calvary to me.

Again, in this fourth verse of the redemption chapter; the Hebrew verbs for "borne" and "carried" (nasa and sabal) are both the same as are used in the eleventh and twelfth verses for the substitutionary bearing of sin, "He shall bear [carry] their iniquities.... And He bare the sin of many." Both words signify a heavy burden, and denote actual substitution, and a complete removal of the thing borne. When Jesus bore our sins, our sicknesses, and our pains, He bore them away, or removed them. Both these words mean "substitution," one bearing another's load. [1]

Jesus literally "bare our sicknesses" (Matthew 8:17). He took our pain and suffering as our substitute in death. In His resurrection He gave us His new life and health. What compassion. What victory, new life and health.

The two words "sorrows" (Heb. "makob") and griefs (Heb. "choli") refer to physical pain, sickness and disease. Included with the transgressions and iniquities, Jesus was wounded and bruised for our full salvation.

The word "makob" literally translated "pain" can be found in Job 33 and Jeremiah 51:8. The literal translation of "griefs" (choli) is disease in 2 Kings 1:8, Job 30:18, 2 Chronicles 21:5. Choli translated literally as "sickness" is found in Deuteronomy 7:15, 1 Kings 17:17 and Isaiah 38:9. With his stripes we are healed" (Isaiah 53:5). The word "stripes" in Hebrew is "kawborah." The literal meaning is to be black and blue. The King James Version translates it five different ways: "blueness" (Proverbs 20:30), "bruise" (Isaiah 1:6, "hurt" (Genesis 4:23), "stripe" (Exodus 21:25), and "wound" (Psalm 38:5).

"Stripes" describes the markings received by a beating with rods (Proverbs 10:13) or with leather straps (Exodus 21:25). In the Greek, "stripes" ("molops") literally means black eye. These two words combined define "stripes" as a bruise (discolored blood under the skin), a mark (welt marks), a wound (an abrasion) and a stripe (a scourging). With this in mind, let us see the deeper meaning of "stripes." After Jesus' arrest, He received a number of beatings

*while being mocked and ridiculed. They "buf-
feted," "smote" and "did strike" Him. The
word "buffet" (Greek, "kolaphezo") means
to strike with a fist (Mark 14:65). To "smote"
(Gk "daero") is to beat until the skin is broken
(Luke 22:63). To "strike" Him (Gk "rapizo")
means to slap with your palm or to smack with
a club, from the root "rapis" meaning "rod,"
(Mark 14:65, John 19:3).[2]*

(LEESER) ...a man of pains, and acquainted with disease....

(BASIC) ... he was a man of sorrows, marked by disease....

(ROTH, BYINGTON) ...Man of pains and familiar with sickness.

(LEESER) But only our disease did He bear Himself, and our pains He carried.

(BASIC) But it was our pain he took, and our diseases were put on him: while to us he seemed as one diseased, on whom God's punishment had come.

(MASORETIC O.T.) Surely our disease He did bear, and our pains He carried....

(ROTH) Yet surely our sicknesses he carried, and as for our pains he bore the burden of them.

(BYINGTON) But in fact it was our sickness he was carrying, our pains he was loaded with.

(SMITH-GOODSPEED) Yet it was our sickness that He

bore, our pains that He carried.

(LEESER) …through His bruises was healing granted to us.

(ROTH) …by his stripes there is healing for us.

(BYINGTON) …the chastisement to give us soundness came on him, and by his stripes we got healing.

(MOF) …the blows that fell to him have brought us healing.

(GOOD NEWS) …We are healed by the punishment he suffered, made whole by the blows he received.

(YOUNG) …by his bruise there is healing to us.

(AMP) …the chastisement needful to obtain peace and well-being for us was upon Him, and with the stripes that wounded Him we are healed and made whole.

CONFESSION: Surely He hath borne my sickness and diseases and carried my pains. He carried my sickness and my pains. He bore them and carried them away. I don't have to bear what he bore for me. I refuse to bear what He bore for me. Satan cannot put on me what Jesus bore for me. By His stripes I am healed. By His stripes I have healing. By his bruises there is healing for me. His punishment has brought me healing. Healing has been granted to me. With the stripes that wounded Him I am healed and made whole. I am made whole by the blows He received. My disease went to the cross with Jesus and died with Him there. Satan,

you're visiting the wrong one. Jesus took my sickness and by His stripes, I am healed.

ISAIAH 53:10 Yet it pleased the Lord to bruise him; he hath put him to grief; when thou shalt make his soul an offering for sin, he shall see his seed, and he shall prolong his days, and the pleasure of the Lord shall prosper in his hand.

(YOUNG) And Jehovah hath delighted to bruise him, He hath made him sick...

(ABV) Yet it pleased Jehovah to crush Him with grievous sickness,

(LEESER) But the Lord was pleased to crush Him through disease...

CONFESSION: Jesus, bruised and crushed with the disease and sickness of all mankind, was wounded, beaten and crucified. He not only became my substitute when His soul was an offering for sin, but God laid on Him every grievous sickness and pain. God took it from me and put it upon Jesus. Thank you, Jesus, for taking it for me so I can be free. Thank you, Father, for loving me that much.

NUMBERS 21:9 And Moses made a serpent of brass and put it upon a pole, and it came to pass that if a serpent had bitten any man, when he beheld the serpent of brass, he lived.

(AMP) ...when he looked to the serpent of bronze [attentively, expectantly, with a steady and absorbing gaze], he lived.

CONFESSION: I am looking to Jesus who took all my pains and diseases to the cross with Him. I see Him becoming a curse for me. I keep looking with expectation and all my attention, focusing on Jesus, my Substitute, with a steady, absorbing gaze. I am absorbing God's healing power into my spirit while I turn my eyes from my body to Jesus' wounded body. I am looking away from all that distracts to Jesus (Heb. 12:2). I draw healing life into my spirit as I look. I expect His life and healing to restore me to health and prevent sickness and disease.

PSALM 103:2, 3 Bless the Lord, O my soul, and forget not all his benefits: Who forgiveth all thine iniquities; who healeth all thy diseases.

(NEB) He pardons all my guilt and heals all my suffering.

(BASIC) ...he takes away all your diseases.

(YOUNG) ...Who is healing all thy diseases.

(MSG) O my soul, bless God, don't forget a single blessing! He forgives your sins—every one. He heals your diseases—every one.

(AMP) Bless (affectionately, gratefully praise) the Lord, O my soul, and forget not [one of] all His benefits—Who

151

forgives [every one of] all your iniquities, Who heals [each one of] all your diseases,

CONFESSION: Bless the Lord, Jehova-Rapha, O my soul. Blessed be God the Father; Lord, I praise You; Lord, I thank you. I praise You for Your benefits. You forgive all my sin, all my faults, all my failures and disobedience. You heal all my diseases, and I thank You for it. Healing belongs to me as part of the New Covenant. Healing is my redemptive right. A benefit is a condition of a contract, not a bonus thrown in extra at the discretion of the employer. Thank You, Father, for healing all my diseases.

MATTHEW 8:16, 17 When the even was come, they brought unto him many that were possessed with devils: and he cast out the spirits with his word, and healed all that were sick: That it might be fulfilled which was spoken by Esaias the prophet, saying, Himself took our infirmities, and bare our sicknesses.

> **Strong's Concordance notes on the word *took*: Greek word is lambano—to get a hold of; *to take* is more violent, to seize or remove, take (away, up).** [3]

(NORLIE) ...He took our infirmities upon Himself, and took away our diseases.

(AMP) ...He Himself took (in order to carry away) our

152

weaknesses and infirmities and bore away our diseases.

(NEB) He took away our illnesses and lifted our diseases from us.

(TRANS) …He took away our illness and carried away our diseases.

(JER) He took our sicknesses away and carried our diseases for us.

(MOF) …He took away our sickness and our diseases he removed.

(NEW LIFE) …He took on Himself our sicknesses and carried away our diseases.

(WUEST, BERKLEY) …carried off our diseases.

CONFESSION: Himself took my infirmities and bare my sicknesses. He carried away my sicknesses. He took them away; He bore them away and removed them. Disease is not mine. Healing is mine. I refuse to bear what Jesus bore for me. I refuse to take what He took for me. Satan, you cannot put disease on me, for Jesus took my infirmities and bore my sicknesses. I refuse to accept sickness. I will not tolerate sickness. Sickness and disease are totally unacceptable. I refuse to accept them. Jesus bore them and I refuse to have them.

GALATIANS 2:20 I am crucified with Christ: nevertheless, I live; yet not I, but Christ liveth in me: and the life which I now live in the flesh, I live by the faith of the Son of God, who loved me and gave Himself for me.

(LAU.) ...Christ took me to the cross with Him, and I died there with Him

(NIV) I have been crucified with Christ.

(DIST) I consider myself as having died and now enjoying a second existence, which is simply Jesus using my body.

CONFESSION: The sick person I was has been crucified with Christ. Now it is no longer I who lives but Christ who lives in me. I see my sickness, disease and pain nailed to the Cross. I died to it and now I am alive, but it is Christ, the Healer, who is living in me. My body is full of the Healer who lives in me. I am now enjoying a second existence, free from sickness and pain in Jesus' name.

CHANGING THE NAME

A wonderful Hebrew commentary called, The Tehillim, has an interesting section with a prayer for a desperately sick person. The Rabbinical authorities would completely change the name of that person. A name was simply added which would allude to life and recovery. For example, the name Raphael, which literally means "God has cured," could be added. They taught this could annul a decree of judgment against a person if he repented.

They would then pray a prayer declaring that the decree issued against this person (stating his/her name) is not valid because that person is a different person now.

Justice has been changed to mercy; death to life; and sickness to complete recovery (patient's new name). Throughout the Bible you can see God change names and give to that person a new name, so that their entire life and identity was changed. Some of them are: Abram to Abraham (father of a multitude); Sarai to Sarah (princess); and Jacob (supplanter, schemer, trickster, swindler) to Israel (prince, contender with God). Jesus changed Saul's name to Paul and Simon Bar-Jonah (reed) to Peter (a large piece of rock).

Through identification with Christ, your former identity was crucified with Him. You are dead to sickness, disease and infirmity. You have a new condition and enjoy a new identity of health and wholeness, according to Galatians 2:20, Galatians 3:13 and 1 Peter 2:24. You have died to the former identity and you are living a new life in Christ. You are now a well person, resisting sickness!

1 PETER 2:24 Who his own self bare our sins in his own body on the tree, that we, being dead to sins, should live unto righteousness: by whose stripes ye were healed.

(20TH CR) ...His bruising was your healing.

(AMP) ...that we might die (cease to exist) to sin and live to righteousness. By His wounds you have been healed.

CONFESSION: By his stripes I was healed. Healing belongs to me. I was healed over 2,000 years ago by the

REDEEMED

stripes Jesus bore. By His stripes I was healed. I'm not trying to get healing. I've got healing, because by His stripes I was healed. I have ceased to exist to sin and sickness!

GALATIANS 3:13 Christ has redeemed us from the curse of the law, being made a curse for us; for it is written, Cursed is everyone that hangeth on a tree.

(TRANS) Christ ransomed us from the curse of the Law by taking that curse upon himself for our sakes....

(WAND) Now, Christ bought us off the curse of the Law at the cost of being accursed for our sakes....

(20TH CR) Christ ransomed us from the curse pronounced in the Law....

(WEYM) Christ has purchased our freedom....

CONFESSION: Christ ransomed and bought me from the curse when He hung on the tree. He took my place and now I am free from everything written in the curse of the law. I am free from all sickness and disease.

The curse for breaking the law in the Old Testament is listed in the following scriptures in Deuteronomy 28. Through Jesus' death, burial and resurrection we have been redeemed from this curse, which includes sickness and disease of every kind.

DEUTERONOMY 28:21-28, 35, 60-61, and 65-67

21 The Lord shall make the pestilence cleave unto thee, until he have consumed thee from off the land, whither thou goest to possess it. 22 The Lord shall smite thee with a consumption, and with a fever, and with an inflammation, and with an extreme burning, and with the sword, and with blasting, and with mildew; and they shall pursue thee until thou perish. 27 The Lord will smite thee with the botch of Egypt, and with the emerods, and with the scab, and with the itch, where of thou canst not be healed. 28 The Lord shall smite thee with madness, and blindness, and astonishment of heart: 35 The Lord shall smite thee in the knees, and in the legs, with a sore botch that cannot be healed, from the sole of thy foot unto the top of thy head. 60 Moreover he will bring upon thee all the diseases of Egypt, which thou wast afraid of; and they shall cleave unto thee. 61 Also every sickness, and every plague, which is not written in the book of this law, them will the Lord bring upon thee, until thou be destroyed. 65 ...a trembling heart, and failing of eyes, and sorrow of mind: 66 And thy life shall hang in doubt before thee; and thou shalt fear day and night, and shalt have none assurance of thy life: 67 In the morning thou shalt say, Would God it were even! and at even thou shalt say, Would God it were morning...

REDEEMED

VERSE 21.
"PESTILENCE"

(GOOD NEWS, BASIC) - disease after disease.

157

God's Healing Word

VERSE 22.

"CONSUMPTION"

(NEW WORLD, TLB) - tuberculosis

(GOOD NEWS) - infectious disease

(BASIC) - wasting disease

"INFLAMMATION"

(SEPT) - cold

(BASIC, MOF, KNOX) - ague (or malarial fever)

"EXTREME BURNING"

(BYINGTON) - influenza

(SMITH-GOODSPEED) - sunstroke

(MOF) - erysipelas

"SWORD"

(JER, BYINGTON) - drought

"BLASTING"

(TLB, OTHERS) - blight

"MILDEW"

(FENTON) - jaundice

(SEPT) - paleness

VERSE 27.

"BOTCH OF EGYPT"

(LEESER) - inflammatory disease

(FENTON, DOUAY, YOUNG) - ulcers

(ROTH, SMITH-GOODSPEED) - sores

(NAB, AMP) - boils

"EMEROLDS"

158

(NIV, AMP) - tumors

(ROTH, LEESER) - hemorrhoids

(RSV, SMITH-GOODSPEED) - ulcers

(KNOX, JER) - swelling in the groin

(GOOD NEWS) - sores

"SCAB"

(TLB, AMP) - scurvy

(NEW WORLD, NAB) - eczema

(NASV, BERKELEY) - incurable itch

(SEPT) - malignant scab

(NIV) - festering sores. "Itch"

(BASIC) - other sorts of skin diseases

(NEW WORLD) - skin eruptions

VERSE 28.

"MADNESS"

(SEPT, BYINGTON) - insanity

(GOOD NEWS) - lose your mind

(KNOX) - distracted

"ASTONISHMENT OF HEART"

(JER) - distraction of mind

(BYINGTON) - imbecility

(SMITH-GOODSPEED) - dismay

(AMP) - dismay of mind and heart

(KNOX) - crazed in thy wits

(LEESER) - confusion of heart

(LIVING BIBLE) - fear and panic

(NAB) - panic

VERSE 35.

"SORE BOTCH"

(FENTON, YOUNG, DOUAY) - ulcer

(ROTH, AMP) - boil

(NAB, NIV) - boils

(BERKELEY, SMITH-GOODSPEED) - sores

(BASIC) - a skin disease

(LEESER) - a sore inflammation

VERSE 61.

(NIV) ...every kind of sickness and disaster not recorded in this Book of the law....

(NAB, CONF)...

any kind of sickness or calamity not mentioned in this Book of the Law...

VERSE 65.

"Trembling heart, and failing of eyes, and sorrow of mind"

(NIV) - an anxious mind, a despairing heart

(JER) - a quaking heart, weary eyes

(BASIC) - a shaking heart

CONFESSION: Christ has redeemed me from the curse of the law. The curse of the law is found in Deuteronomy 28. It is the curse for breaking God's law. It includes sickness, as the scriptures above show.

Christ bought me back, brought me back, and set me free from the curse of the law. Sickness and disease are part of the curse of the law; therefore Christ has redeemed me from sickness. I am liberated, I am ransomed, I am free from disease. I am redeemed from every disease written in the curse of the law. "I am redeemed from (say the specific condition or sickness)_____." I am redeemed from every disease that is not written in the Book of the Law. Christ has redeemed me—bought me back, brought me back, and set me free from all sickness and disease.

MALACHI 4:2 But unto you that fear my name shall the Sun of righteousness arise with healing in his wings; and ye shall go forth, and grow up as calves of the stall.

(AMP)...like calves [released] from the stall and leap for joy.

CONFESSION: The Son of righteousness has arisen, having conquered sickness and Satan. There is healing in His wings. That healing is beaming into me now by His Word. I am trusting beneath His healing wings.

End Notes
1. Bosworth, FF, *Christ the Healer*
2. Prince, Joseph, *http://vitaminforthesoul.blogspot.com/2008/04/jesus-bore-your-diseases.html*
3. Strong, James, The New Strong Exhaustive Condordance of the Bible, G2983

Faith moves God. Faith moves mountains. But faith won't move anything until it moves you. The first part of you that your faith will move is your mouth.

- Mark Hankins

CHAPTER ELEVEN

Act on the Word

MATTHEW 8:5-10, 13 And when Jesus was entered into Capernaum, there came unto him a centurion, beseeching him, And saying, Lord, my servant lieth at home sick of the palsy, grievously tormented. And Jesus saith unto him, I will come and heal him. The centurion answered and said, Lord, I am not worthy that thou shouldest come under my roof: but speak the word only, and my servant shall be healed. For I am a man under authority, having soldiers under me: and I say to this man, Go, and he goeth; and to another, Come, and he cometh; and to my servant, Do this, and he doeth it. When Jesus heard it, he marvelled, and said to them that followed, Verily I say unto you, I have not found so great faith, no, not in Israel. And Jesus said unto the centurion, Go thy way; and as thou hast believed, so be it done unto thee. And his servant was healed in the selfsame hour.

(MSG) "...Just give the order and my servant will be fine. I'm a man who takes orders and give orders. I tell one soldier, 'Go,' and he goes; to another, 'Come,' and he comes; to my slave, 'Do this,' and he does it." Then Jesus turned to the captain and said, "Go. What you believed could happen has happened." At that moment his servant became well.

(GNT) Just give the order, and my servant will get well. When Jesus heard this, he was surprised and said to the people following him, "I tell you, I have never found anyone in Israel with faith like this." Then Jesus said to the officer, "Go home, and what you believe will be done for you." And the officer's servant was healed that very moment.

(GWT) The officer responded, "Sir, I don't deserve to have you come into my house. But just give a command, and my servant will be healed." Jesus was amazed when he heard this. He said to those who were following him, "I can guarantee this truth: I haven't found faith as great as this in anyone in Israel.... Jesus told the officer, "Go! What you believed will be done for you." And at that moment the servant was healed.

CONFESSION: The Word of God is the final authority in my life. Jesus is always the same and He is looking for faith. The Word of healing has been sent to me from Jesus Christ. Like the centurion, I say, "Speak the Word only." It is done the moment I hear the com-

mand from Jesus. What I believed could happen has happened.

MATTHEW 9:6-8 But that ye may know that the Son of man hath power on earth to forgive sins, (then saith he to the sick of the palsy,) Arise, take up thy bed, and go unto thine house. And he arose, and departed to his house.

(MSG) At this he turned to the paraplegic and said, "Get up. Take your bed and go home." And the man did it.

(GWT) Then he said to the paralyzed man, "Get up, pick up your stretcher, and go home."So the man got up and went home.

(CEVUK) So Jesus said to the man, "Get up! Pick up your mat and go on home." The man got up and went home.

CONFESSION: Jesus has the power to forgive sins as well as heal bodies. The same faith that saves me heals me. My act of faith is to do what Jesus tells me in His Word. I act on the Word of God. I am forgiven in my spirit and I am healed in my body.

MATTHEW 12:13 Then saith he to the man, Stretch forth thine hand. And he stretched it forth; and it was restored whole, like as the other.

(GWT) Then he said to the man, "Hold out your hand." The man held it out, and it became normal again, as healthy as the other.

ACTION

(NLT) Then he said to the man, "Hold out your hand." So the man held out his hand, and it was restored, just like the other one!

(CEB) And it was made healthy, just like the other one.

(OJB) And it was restored to health, as sound as the other hand.

CONFESSION: Jesus commanded the man to do something that was impossible to the natural mind, but he believed and acted on the Word of restoration. This action got him results. I act on the Word of God. Jesus is speaking through His Word today, right now, to me. I believe and act today on His Word. He is speaking to me now, "Act on the Word! Faith is an act!"

ACTS 3:6-9 Then Peter said, Silver and gold have I none; but such as I have give I thee: In the name of Jesus Christ of Nazareth rise up and walk. And he took him by the right hand, and lifted him up: and immediately his feet and ankle bones received strength. And he leaping up stood, and walked, and entered with them into the temple, walking, and leaping, and praising God. And all the people saw him walking and praising God:

(AMP) Then he took hold of the man's right hand with a firm grip and raised him up. And at once his feet and ankle bones became strong and steady, And leaping forth he stood and began to walk, and he went into

166

the temple with them, walking and leaping and praising God.

(CEB) Jumping up, he began to walk around. He entered the temple with them, walking, leaping, and praising God.

(MSG) In an instant his feet and ankles became firm. He jumped to his feet and walked.

CONFESSION: The Name of Jesus is powerful. He is the same now as He was in the book of Acts. I obey the command of faith to believe in the Name of Jesus to heal me. I will rise, believe and act on the command of faith. I shall walk, leap and praise God with all that is in me.

ACTS 3:16 And his name, through faith in his name, hath made this man strong, whom ye see and know; yea, the faith which is by him hath given him this perfect soundness in the presence of you all.

CONFESSION: His name, through faith in His name makes me whole, gives me perfect soundness and makes me strong. The name of Jesus is greater than sickness. He conquered sickness. I speak His name, Jesus, to my body now. I declare I am healed and well in Jesus' name. *(Name your condition or sickness)*_____ **must bow to Jesus' Name. My body is made whole in Jesus' name.**

ACTS 14:8-10 And there sat a certain man at Lystra, impotent in his feet, being a cripple from his mother's womb, who never had walked: The same heard Paul speak: who stedfastly beholding him, and perceiving that he had faith to be healed, Said with a loud voice, Stand upright on thy feet. And he leaped and walked.

(AMP) He was listening to Paul as he talked, and [Paul] gazing intently at him and observing that he had faith to be healed, Shouted at him, saying, Stand erect on your feet! And he leaped up and walked.

(MSG) ...and Paul, looking him in the eye, saw that he was ripe for God's work, ready to believe. So he said, loud enough for everyone to hear, "Up on your feet!" The man was up in a flash—jumped up and walked around as if he'd been walking all his life.

(WUEST) ...and having seen that he was having faith to be healed, said in a great voice, Stand upright on your feet. And he leaped up with a single bound and went to walking about.

CONFESSION: My faith is activated when I hear the gospel. The power of the gospel gives me faith to be healed. I receive the command of faith to act upon what I've heard. My faith is from my heart and I respond quickly to the command to act upon what I know and what I've heard. I act on what I've heard and the Spirit of God confirms God's Word with signs following. Hallelujah, I am healed.

Shout to testify your faith in God's promise, and thankfulness for this glorious mercy; to encourage yourselves and brethren, and to strike terror into your enemies.

- John Wesley

CHAPTER TWELVE

Use Your Authority and Receive Your Healing

> In Mark 11:23, Jesus used three different Greek words to explain the speaking part of faith. The first *say* is the Greek word *epo*, which means command. It shows the authority of the believer. The second reference to speaking that Jesus used was the word *saith*. This word in the Greek is *laleo*, which means to speak out, use your own voice, and be bold. The third reference to speaking is also the word *saith*. However, this Greek word is *lego,* which means a systematic set discourse. The phrase, "he shall have whatsoever he saith," means a <u>journey</u> or that you are <u>on the way</u>.

AUTHORITY

MARK 11:23 For verily I say unto you, That whosoever shall say unto this mountain, Be thou removed, and be thou cast into the sea; and shall not doubt in his heart, but shall believe that those things which he saith shall come to pass; he shall have whatsoever he saith.

(RIEU) ...if any man orders this mountain to be removed and cast into the sea, and does not waver in his heart, but believes that what he says is done, it will be done for him.

(NORLIE) "...Move! Throw yourself into the sea..."

(KNOX) ...has no hesitation in his heart, but is sure that what he says is to come about...

(DOUAY) ...shall not stagger in his heart...

(JOHNSON) Truly, anyone who speaks to that mountain yonder saying, "Dump yourself in the lake," and does not become separated from the statement he makes - that person will actualize his statement. When anyone's expression in prayer is congruent with his inner being, his desire will be actualized.

CONFESSION: According to the teaching of Jesus, I speak to the mountain of (name your condition or sickness)_____and command it to go. I order it to be removed, to move out of my body and to disappear. I do not doubt in my heart because I am a believer. I will not be separated from this statement. It is being actualized because I do not stagger in my heart or entertain any doubt. I see the mountain of sickness disappearing into the sea of God's mercy.

MATTHEW 16:19 And I will give unto thee the keys of the kingdom of heaven: and whatsoever thou shalt bind on earth shall be bound in heaven: and whatsoever thou shalt loose on earth shall be loosed in heaven.

(AMP) I will give you the keys of the kingdom of heaven; and whatever you bind (declare to be improper and unlawful) on earth must be what is already bound in heaven; and whatever you loose (declare lawful) on earth must be what is already loosed in heaven.

(MSG) And that's not all. You will have complete and free access to God's kingdom, keys to open any and every door: no more barriers between heaven and earth, earth and heaven. A yes on earth is yes in heaven. A no on earth is no in heaven.

CONFESSION: Jesus has given me the keys of the kingdom of heaven. I have been given the right, privilege and responsibility to exercise my authority as a believer in Christ. I release my authority as a believer with words of faith. I declare that (name your condition or sickness)_____is now bound. Every assignment from the powers of darkness is unlawful and bound. I declare that the door to divine healing and health is open. It is God's will for me to be well. He says, "Yes" to my health and healing. I declare, "Yes!" to the will of Heaven in my life and I shout, "No!" to what Jesus died to redeem me from!

AUTHORITY

173

LUKE 13:11-13, 16 And, behold, there was a woman which had a spirit of infirmity eighteen years, and was bowed together, and could in no wise lift up herself. And when Jesus saw her, he called her to him, and said unto her, Woman, thou art loosed from thine infirmity. And he laid his hands on her: and immediately she was made straight, and glorified God. And ought not this woman, being a daughter of Abraham, whom Satan hath bound, lo, these eighteen years, be loosed from this bond on the Sabbath day?

(AMP) ...an infirmity caused by a spirit [a demon of sickness]

(PLAIN) ...had a disease caused by an evil spirit; she was bent double and altogether unable to hold herself up.

(DOUAY) ...thou art delivered.

(SMITH-GOODSPEED, CONFRATERNITY) ...a sickness caused by a spirit.

(WUEST) ...A woman had a spirit that caused an infirmity eighteen years and was completely bent together by a curvature of the spine, and was not able to raise herself up at all.

(NASNT) ...you are freed from your sickness.

(MARSHALL) ...thou hast been loosed.

(BASIC) ...you are made free from your disease.

(NIV) ...you are set free from your infirmity.

(NORLIE) ...you are now rid of your infirmity.

174

(PL ENG) …you are freed from your disease.

(JORDAN) …Lady, you have been freed from your weakness.

(WORRELL) …Woman, you have been loosed from your infirmity.

(CONDON) …Your bondage is at end.

(WILLIAMS) …at once she straightened herself up and burst into praising God.

(ROTH) …was there not a needs be – be that she be loosed...

(WADE) And ought not this woman, a descendant of Abraham as she is, whose power of movement Satan has fettered actually for eighteen years, to have been released from such fetters on the day of the Sabbath?

(BARCLAY) …For eighteen years Satan has fettered her. Is it not right that she should be liberated from her fetters?

(BASIC) …And is it not right for this daughter of Abraham, who has been in the power of Satan for eighteen years, to be made free on the Sabbath?

(NORLIE) But this woman, a daughter of Abraham, who has been in the bondage of Satan - think of it! — for eighteen years, should not have the right to be released from her bonds because it is the Sabbath?

CONFESSION: Satan can't bind me with sickness. I have been delivered from Satan's dominion and translated into the kingdom of the Son of God (Co-

175

lossians 1:13). Sickness is ungodly. Sickness is of the devil. Satan, you can't put sickness on me. Who do think you are? You are a defeated foe. Jesus stripped you of your authority over me (Colossians 2:15, Hebrews 2:14). You can't do this to me. I resist you in Jesus' name. I am delivered. I am free—I have been loosed. I am no longer fettered. I am rid of my infirmity. My bondage is at an end! It is right for me to be completely free for Abraham's blessings are mine in Christ. (Galatians 3:14, 29). Healing is part of the covenant. I am under the covenant. Healing is mine. Healing belongs to me. It is my rightful possession. I have a right to be released. Satan, I demand my rights now. Take your filthy hands off my body!

JAMES 5:15-16 And the prayer of faith shall save the sick, and the Lord shall raise him up; and if he have committed sins, they shall be forgiven him. Confess your faults one to another and pray one for another, that ye may be healed. The effectual fervent prayer of a righteous man availeth much.

(BASIC) And by the prayer of faith the man who is ill will be made well.

(WADE) And the prayer offered in faith will restore the sufferer to health, and the Lord will raise him from his sick-bed.

(TLB) ...The earnest prayer of a righteous man has great power and wonderful results.

(**ADAMS**) ...has very powerful effects.

(**AMP**) ...The earnest (heartfelt, continued) prayer of a righteous man makes tremendous power available (dynamic in its working).

CONFESSION: The prayer of faith has made me whole. The Lord is raising me up. I cannot stay down. I believe I received when I prayed, and my faith makes me whole. I believe I have received my healing. Earnest, heartfelt and continued prayer makes tremendous power available to me now. It is working dynamically in me now, effecting a healing and cure in my body.

ACTS 10:38 How God anointed Jesus of Nazareth with the Holy Ghost and with power: who went about doing good, and healing all that were oppressed of the devil; for God was with him.

(**MOF**) ...all who were harassed by the devil....

(**NIV, PL ENG**)...healing all who were under the power of the devil....

(**RIEU**)...healing everyone in the devil's clutches....

(**BARCLAY**)...curing all those who were under the tyranny of the devil....

(**NEW BERKELEY**) ...healing all that were overpowered by the devil....

(**WEYM**) ...was curing all who were being continually oppressed by the devil...

177

AUTHORITY

(JORDAN) …God equipped him with the Holy Spirit and power, who passed through our midst acting nobly and healing all those who were lorded over by the devil.…

(PHILLIPS) …healing all who suffered from the devil's power.…

(CONC) …who passed through as a benefactor and healer of all those who are tyrannized over by the adversary.…

(AMP) …harassed and oppressed by [the power of] the devil.…

CONFESSION: Sickness is oppression of the devil. Satan can't oppress me with sickness, for I have been delivered from his authority (Colossians 1:13). Satan can't oppress me. I have authority to tread on Satan and demons and all the power the enemy possesses (Luke 10:19). I tread on sickness. Satan, you can't lord over me with foul disease. You can't do this to me. Sickness, you can't do this to me. You are visiting the wrong one. Healing is mine. The power that raised Jesus from the dead is at work in me. It is healing power because He is the Lord that healeth. Healing power is at work in me and I am free.

ROMANS 8:2 For the law of the Spirit of life in Christ Jesus hath made me free from the law of sin and death.

(KNOX) The spiritual principle of life has set me free, in

Christ Jesus, from the principle of sin and death.

(TRANS) For the principle of spiritual life in Christ Jesus has liberated me from the principle of sin and death.

(AMP) ...[the law of our new being]...

CONFESSION: I have been set free from the power and principle of sin and death. Sickness and disease are a manifestation of sin and death. The power of life and health in Christ Jesus is greater than the power of sickness and disease. That power is effectually at work in me now. I am free from the law and power of sin and death.

ROMANS 8:11 But if the Spirit of him that raised up Jesus from the dead dwells in you, He that raised up Christ from the dead shall also quicken your mortal bodies by His Spirit that dwelleth in you.

(WAY) If the Spirit of God, of Him who raised Jesus from the dead, has its home in you, then He who raised Messiah Jesus from the dead will thrill with a new life your very bodies - those mortal bodies of yours - by the agency of His own Spirit, which now has its home in you.

(GOODSPEED) If the Spirit of him who raised Jesus from the dead has taken possession of you, he who raised Christ Jesus from the dead will also give your mortal bodies life through his Spirit that has taken possession of you.

AUTHORITY

CONFESSION: The Spirit of God is residing in me. The Spirit of God is making His home in my spirit. The Spirit of Jehovah–Rapha is in me, giving life to my body. The Spirit of the Lord that healeth is creating life, supplying life in my body, making it whole. The life of Jehovah-Rapha is being applied to my body by His Spirit who dwells in me. The life of God is destroying disease in my body now.

1 CORINTHIANS 6:15, 19, and 20 Know ye not that your bodies are the members of Christ? Shall I then take the members of Christ, and make them the members of an harlot? God forbid. What? Know ye not that your body is the temple of the Holy Ghost, which is in you, which ye have of God, and ye are not your own? For ye are bought with a price: therefore glorify God in your body, and in your spirit, which are God's.

CONFESSION: My body wasn't made for sin but for the Lord. My body is a member of Christ. My body belongs to Christ. Satan cannot make Christ's body sick. Satan, how dare you trespass on God's property? Take your hands off God's property in Jesus' name. My body is the temple of Jehova–Rapha, the Lord that healeth. He is in me, healing me now, for He is the Lord that healeth me. I have been bought with a price. Jesus' blood cleansed me from all sins, and by His stripes, my body is healed. I glorify God in my

body. I refuse to allow sickness in my body in Jesus' name. You foul disease, take your hands off my body in Jesus' name. The Lord is for my body and my body is for the Lord (1 Cor. 6:13).

EPHESIANS 4:27 Neither give place to the devil.

(**WILLIAMS**) stop giving the devil a chance.

(**BARCLAY**) Give the devil no place or opportunity in your life.

(**TRANS**) …and do not give the devil a chance.

(**JORDAN**) …don't give in one inch to the devil.

CONFESSION: I refuse to give place to the devil. Sickness and disease are of the devil. I refuse to give place to sickness and disease. Satan, you can't put that on my body. You can't, you can't, you can't. I say NO and I mean NO. No sickness or plague comes nigh my dwelling. You have the wrong address. I will not give in one inch. Satan, you have no place in my body. I belong to God. Sickness, you have no choice but to go because I'm not giving you a chance. Get out now.

COLOSSIANS 1:12 Giving thanks unto the Father which hath made us meet to be partakers of the inheritance of the saints in light.

(**SMITH-GOODSPEED**)…thank the Father, Who has entitled you to share the lot of God's people in the realm of light.

AUTHORITY

(**NEW BERKELEY**) ...who has qualified you for your share in the inheritance of the saints in the light.

(**ROTH**) ...the Father that hath made you sufficient for your share....

(**GODBEY**) ...who has made us worthy....

(**NOLI**) ...he enabled us to share the inheritance of the saints who live in the light.

(**TLB**) ...to share all the wonderful things that belong to those who live in the kingdom of light.

CONFESSION: I am qualified, entitled, worthy and able to partake of my inheritance in Christ. Healing belongs to me (Psalm 103:3). I refuse to be beaten out of my inheritance.

COLOSSIANS 1:13 Who hath delivered us from the power of darkness, and hath translated us into the kingdom of his dear Son.

(**SMITH-GOODSPEED**) He has rescued us from the dominion of darkness, and has transferred us into the realm of his dear Son.

(**PL ENG**) He has freed us from the power of darkness and carried us away into the kingdom of his beloved Son.

(**CONY**) For He has delivered us from the dominion of darkness, and translated us into the kingdom of His beloved Son.

(**WADE**) For God has rescued us from the dominance exercised by the powers of Spiritual Darkness, and transferred us to the Dominion of His Son — the Object of His love.

(TLB) For he has rescued us out of the darkness and gloom of Satan's kingdom and brought us into the kingdom of His dear Son.

CONFESSION: I have been delivered from the authority of darkness. I have been delivered from Satan's authority and dominion. Sickness is of the devil. Satan, I've been delivered from your authority. You can't put sickness on me. I have passed out of your jurisdiction into the kingdom of the Son of God. I am a citizen in the kingdom of Jehovah-Rapha, the Lord that healeth me. I have been transplanted into the kingdom of His Son.

COLOSSIANS 1:14 In whom we have redemption through His blood, even the forgiveness of sins.

(SMITH-GOODSPEED) ...by whom we have been ransomed from captivity....

(CONBEARE) ...in Whom we have our redemption....

(WAY) ...in whom we have our ransoming, The remission of our sins.

CONFESSION: I am redeemed by the blood of Jesus. I am no longer a captive of sickness. I am delivered, set free from the power of Satan, his works and dominion. I am forgiven and healed by the blood of Jesus.

AUTHORITY

LUKE 10:19 Behold, I give unto you power to tread on serpents and scorpions, and over all the power of the enemy: and nothing shall by any means hurt you.

(**NORLIE**) I have given you authority to trample on serpents and scorpions and all the might of the satanic foe, and nothing will harm you in any way.

(**KNOX**) …I have given you the right to….

(**AMP**) Behold! I have given you authority and power to trample upon serpents and scorpions, and (physical and mental strength and ability) over all the power that the enemy (possesses) and nothing shall in any way harm you.

(**CONDON**) Yes, I have given you power to trample every evil underfoot, to counter all might of the enemy: nothing whatever shall harm you.

(**AUTHENTIC**) I have indeed invested you with power to stamp on snakes and scorpions….

CONFESSION: Sickness is a power of the devil (Acts 10:38). I trample on all the power of the devil. I trample on disease. I stomp on disease. I tread every evil underfoot. The Lord Jesus Christ gave me authority over all power of the enemy. I have authority over sickness. Sickness, I trample on you. I tread on you. I stomp on you. Get out, get out, get out. You have no right to dominate me. Get out of my body in Jesus' name. Sickness and disease are under my feet because

I am seated with Christ above all the power of the enemy (Ephesians 2:6).

JAMES 4:7 Submit yourselves therefore to God. Resist the devil, and he will flee from you.

> (BARCLAY) So then, accept the authority of God. Take a stand against the devil, and he will run away from you.
>
> (NEB) Stand up to the devil and he will turn and run.
>
> (WUEST) Stand immovable against the onset of the devil and he will flee from you.
>
> (BASIC) …be ruled by God; but make war on the Evil One and he will be put to flight before you.

CONFESSION: I submit to God and to His Word which is His will. I accept the authority of God and His Word. I submit to God's Word. I resist disease. You can't do this to my body. Remove yourself. You must flee from my body now.

1 PETER 5:8, 9 Be sober, be vigilant; because your adversary the devil, as a roaring lion, walketh about, seeking whom he may devour: Whom resist steadfast in the faith, knowing that the same afflictions are accomplished in your brethren that are in the world.

> (BARCLAY) You must resist him with a rock-like faith….
>
> (WUEST) Stand immovable against his onset, solid as a rock in your faith….

AUTHORITY

(AMP) ...be firm in faith (against his onset) — rooted, established, strong immovable, and determined....

CONFESSION: I stand immovable against the onset of sickness in Jesus' name. I refuse to accept it! I am strong in faith and as immovable as a rock!

1 JOHN 3:8 He that committeth sin is of the devil, for the devil sinneth from the beginning. For this purpose the Son of God was manifested, that he might destroy the works of the devil.

(AMP) The reason the Son of God was made manifest (visible) was to undo (destroy, loosen and dissolve) the works the devil (has done).

(YOUNG) ...that he might break up the works the devil.

(BASIC) ...and the Son of God was seen on earth, so that he might put an end to the works of the evil one.

(WAND) ...that he might neutralize what the devil had done.

(JORDAN) ...that he might break up the devil's doings.

(JER) ...to lead a sinful life is to belong to the devil, since the devil was a sinner from the beginning. It was to undo all that the devil has done that the Son of God appeared.

(PHILLIPS) Now the Son of God came to the earth with the express purpose of liquidating the devil's activities.

(CONC) ...that He should be annulling the acts of the adversary.

CONFESSION: Sickness is a work of the devil. Jesus came to destroy the works of the devil. Sickness has been dissolved, broken up, annulled, undone and liquidated, as far as I am concerned. Jesus put sickness to an end for me. The activities of the devil have been liquidated.

PHILIPPIANS 2:13 For it is God which worketh in you both to will and to do of his good pleasure.

(AMP) [Not in your own strength] for it is God Who is all the while effectually at work in you [energizing and creating in you the power and desire], both to will and to work for His good pleasure and satisfaction and delight.

(BERKELEY) God is the energizer within you.

CONFESSION: God, Jehovah–Rapha, my Healer is working in my spirit, soul, and body. He is creating healing in every part of my body. He is energizing me by His power which is effectually working in me. My body is being energized! New life is being created in my entire body (or name the specific areas of your body)_____.

MARK 16:17, 18 And these signs shall follow them that believe; In my name shall they cast out devils; they shall speak with new tongues; They shall take up serpents; and

AUTHORITY

187

if they drink any deadly thing, it shall not hurt them; they shall lay hands on the sick, and they shall recover.

(WILLIAMS) …By using my name they will drive out demons….

(BARCLAY) These are the visible demonstrations of the action of God which will accompany the life of those who believe. By using my name they will eject demons….

(MOF) …for those who believe, these miracles will follow… .

(SMITH-GOODSPEED) …with my name they will drive out demons.

(WEYM) …making use of my Name they shall expel demons.

(TRANS) Wherever men believe, these signs will be found….

(WADE) By the use of my name they will expel demons; they will speak rapturously in strange languages… They will place their hands upon invalids, and they will be restored to health.

CONFESSION: The name of Jesus is greater than sickness. Jesus conquered sin, sickness and Satan. I command disease to leave my body. Satan, take your hands off my body. I cast you out in Jesus' name. You can't do this to me. In the name of Jesus, I am free.

Abide in me, and I in you. As the branch cannot bear fruit of itself, except it abide in the vine; no more can ye, except ye abide in me.

- John 15:4, 5

CHAPTER THIRTEEN

Maintain Your Healing

MAINTAIN YOUR HEALING
THROUGH THE WORD

REVELATION 12:11 And they overcame him by the blood of the Lamb, and by the word of their testimony; and they loved not their lives unto the death.

(ISR98) And they overcame him because of the Blood of the Lamb, and because of the Word of their witness, and they did not love their lives to the death.

(MSG) They defeated him through the blood of the Lamb and the bold word of their witness.

(GNBDK) ....by the truth which they proclaimed;

CONFESSION: I overcome Satan, sickness, accusation, fear, and anxiety by the blood of the Lamb and the word of my testimony. I boldly proclaim the truth. I release my faith in the blood of Jesus. I am victori-

191

ous. I am not afraid. I will live my life for the glory of God.

GALATIANS 2:20 I am crucified with Christ: nevertheless I live; yet not I, but Christ liveth in me: and the life which I now live in the flesh I live by the faith of the Son of God, who loved me, and gave himself for me.

(LAU) …Christ took me to the cross with Him, and I died there with Him.

(BARCLAY) ...True, my physical life goes on, but its mainspring is faith in the Son of God.

(DEANE) ...my life is mystically united to his...

(ABBREV. BIBLE) I was crucified with Christ so that he might live in me....

(DIST) I consider myself as having died and now enjoying a second existence, which is simply Jesus using my body.

(NOLI) Now it is not my old self, but Christ Himself who lives in me.

CONFESSION: I was crucified with Christ. I died with Him to sickness and disease. Christ the Healer lives in me. Healing is in me. Christ in me heals me.

JOHN 15:4, 5 Abide in me, and I in you. As the branch cannot bear fruit of itself, except it abide in the vine; no more can ye, except ye abide in me. I am the vine; ye are the branches: he that abideth in me, and I in him, the same bringeth forth much fruit: for without me, ye can do nothing.

(**NEW LIFE**) Get your life from Me and I will live in you. No branch can give fruit by itself. It has to get life from the vine. You are able to give fruit only when you have life from Me. I am the vine and you are the branches. Get your life from Me.

(**PHILLIPS**) You must go on growing in Me and I will grow in you. For just as the branch cannot bear any fruit unless it shares the life of the vine, so you can produce nothing unless you go on growing in me. I am the vine itself; you are the branches. It is the man who shares my life and whose life I share who proves fruitful. For the plain fact is that apart from me you can do nothing at all.

(**AMP**) Dwell in Me, and I will dwell in you. [Live in Me, and I will live in you.] Just as no branch can bear fruit of itself without abiding in (being vitally united to) the vine, neither can you bear fruit unless you abide in Me.

CONFESSION: I am in union with Christ. My spirit is in union with Christ the Healer. I draw out His healing power and it is manifested in my body. I am one with the healing Vine. I am in union with the healing Christ. I have His life and health in me. His Word dwells in me and I dwell in it. I maintain a living relationship with Christ, my Healer, through abiding in His Word.

MAINTAIN

MAINTAIN YOUR HEALING THROUGH YOUR CONFESSION

NAHUM 1:8, 9 But with an overrunning flood he will make an utter end of the place thereof...he will make an utter end: affliction shall not rise up the second time.

(AMP) But with an overrunning flood He will make a full end...He will make a full end...affliction shall not rise up the second time.

(NKJV) But with an overflowing flood He will make an utter end of its place...He will make an utter end of it. Affliction will not rise up a second time.

CONFESSION: I boldly declare that I have been healed by the power of God! His Word and His Power have completely made a complete end of (name of sickness or condition)_____. It shall not return again. I am not afraid of a recurrence. It is completely gone and I am completely healed and made whole!

MICAH 7:8 Rejoice not against me, O mine enemy! When I fall, I shall arise; when I sit in darkness, the Lord shall be a light unto me.

(CEB) Do not rejoice over me, my enemy, because when I fall, I will rise; if I sit in darkness, the LORD is my light.

(CPDV) You, my enemy, should not rejoice over me because I have fallen. I will rise up, when I sit in darkness. The Lord is my light.

CONFESSION: I am confident and I rejoice! Ha, ha, ha! The Lord is my light and salvation so whom shall I fear? I'm not afraid of sickness or disease! The Lord, the Sun of Righteousness, has arisen with healing in His wings and I am raised up with Christ to new life and health.

ISAIAH 26:13, 14 O Lord, our God, other lords beside thee have had dominion over us: but by thee only will we make mention of thy name. They are dead, they shall not live; they are deceased, they shall not rise: therefore hast thou visited and destroyed them, and made all their memory to perish.

(AMP) O Lord, our God, other masters besides You have ruled over us, but we will acknowledge and mention Your name only. They [the former tyrant masters] are dead, they shall not live and reappear; they are powerless ghosts, they shall not rise and come back. Therefore You have visited and made an end of them and caused every memory of them [every trace of their supremacy] to perish.

(MSG) O God, our God, we've had other masters rule us, but you're the only Master we've ever known. The dead don't talk, ghosts don't walk, Because you've said, "Enough—that's all for you," and wiped them off the books.

(CEV) Those enemies are now dead and can never live again. You have punished them— they are destroyed, completely forgotten.

CONFESSION: I declare that the enemies of sickness and disease are dead, powerless ghosts. Jesus took my place on the cross. He was wounded, bruised, chastised and bore stripes on His back for my sickness and pain. Jesus has triumphed over every enemy, over all spirits of infirmity and has destroyed their power to harm me. He said, "It is finished!" I say to sickness and disease that it is finished! Every memory—every trace of your supremacy has perished and is completely forgotten. The sickness or disease will not reappear. It is a powerless ghost! (Name your sickness or condition) _____is wiped off the books! Ha, ha, ha! Jehovah Rapha, my Healer, I acknowledge and reverence Your Name only. You are my Lord and Healer.

PSALM 118:17 I shall not die, but live, and declare the works of the Lord.

(GWT) I will not die, but I will live and tell what the Lord has done.

(MSG) I didn't die. I lived! And now I'm telling the world what God did.

CONFESSION: I shall not die, but I shall live long and live strong to tell the world about what God has done for me. What He has done for me, He will do for

anyone who believes His Word and trusts in His power and grace. I did not die! I am living to tell everyone I meet what God has done for me!

MAINTAIN YOUR HEALING
THROUGH REJOICING

PROVERBS 17:22 A merry heart doeth good like a medicine: but a broken spirit drieth the bones.

(GOOD NEWS) Being cheerful keeps you healthy.

(SMITH-GOODSPEED) A happy heart is a healing medicine….

(BASIC) A glad heart makes a healthy body….

(MOF) A glad heart helps and heals….

(JER) A glad heart is excellent medicine, a spirit depressed wastes the bones away.

(KNOX) A cheerful heart makes a quick recovery; it is crushed spirits that waste a man's frame.

(FENTON) The best medicine is a cheerful heart.

(ROTH) A joyful heart worketh an excellent cure….

(LIVING BIBLE) …a broken spirit makes one sick.

(AMP) A happy heart is good medicine and a cheerful mind works healing....

CONFESSION: Ha, ha, ha, ha, ha, ha, ha, ha! I have a merry heart. Sickness can't dominate me. Satan can't dominate me. What do you think you're trying to do, devil? You can't put sickness on me. Ha, ha, ha, ha,

197

ha, ha, ha, ha! I have a merry heart. I'm full of joy. A merry heart works like a medicine. God's medicine is working in me now!

1 PETER 1:8, 9 Whom having not seen, ye love; in whom, though now ye see him not, yet believing, ye rejoice with joy unspeakable and full of glory: Receiving the end of your faith, even the salvation of your souls.

(AMP) Without having seen Him, you love Him; though you do not [even] now see Him, you believe in Him and exult and thrill with inexpressible and glorious (triumphant, heavenly) joy. [At the same time] you receive the result (outcome, consummation) of your faith, the salvation of your souls.

(NEB) ...you are transported with a joy too great for words, while you reap the harvest of your faith, that is, salvation for your souls.

CONFESSION: My joy is full because I believe I have receiving my healing. I rejoice with heavenly, triumphant joy at the same time I receive the outcome of my faith, what I have believed God for. My rejoicing is an act of faith. It's mine, I have it now. While I rejoice, I am reaping the harvest of my faith. I see myself whole and strong. Thank you! My joy is a container for the glory of God that quickens and gives life to my body.

MAINTAIN YOUR HEALING
THROUGH GOD'S PEACE

MARK 5:34 And he said unto her, Daughter, thy faith hath made thee whole; go in peace, and be whole of thy plague.

(AMP) And He said to her, Daughter, your faith (your trust and confidence in Me, springing from faith in God) has restored you to health. Go in (into) peace and be continually healed and freed from your [distressing bodily] disease.

CONFESSION: I have laid hold of healing virtue in Christ. He and His Word are one. As I speak it and act upon it, I lay hold of the power to heal me. Like the woman who touched Jesus, I continue to speak my faith and lay hold upon the power of God. Then, I keep myself in the peace of God where I stay completely healed. The same faith that healed me will make me whole.

PHILIPPIANS 4:6 Be careful for nothing; but in every thing by prayer and supplication with thanksgiving let your requests be made known unto God.

(AMP) Do not fret or have any anxiety about anything, but in every circumstance and in everything, by prayer and petition (definite requests), with thanksgiving, continue to make your wants known to God.

(MSG) Don't fret or worry. Instead of worrying, pray. Let petitions and praises shape your worries into prayers,

199

letting God know your concerns. Before you know it, a sense of God's wholeness, everything coming together for good, will come and settle you down. It's wonderful what happens when Christ displaces worry at the center of your life.

CONFESSION: I am in union with Christ my Healer. I have His faith and His power is working in me now. I do not worry or have anxiety, but fully trust God as my Healer. I am continually freed from disease and pain. Body – be at peace! Every cell and organ in my body is surrounded by the peace of God. Peace means that nothing is missing and nothing is broken. I am continually healed and freed from (name the condition or sickness_____.

The peace of God is guarding my mind, will and emotions. I am dwelling in Christ, in His peace. It is guarding my heart and my mind in Christ Jesus. My mind is at rest while God's healing is working from my spirit to my body. Thank you Jesus, my Prince of Peace, for complete healing in my body.

PSALM 119:165 Great peace have they which love thy law: and nothing shall offend them.
CONFESSION: I love God's Word and I act upon it. I experience great peace and shall not be offended, but will walk in the God-kind of love. God's peace brings me complete wholeness, nothing missing and nothing broken.

God is on my side,
For the blood has been applied.
Every need shall be supplied,
Nothing shall be denied.

So I enter into rest,
I know that I am blessed.
I have passed the test and
I will get God's best.

-Trina Hankins

The blood of Jesus purges me of every
defilement of the enemy.
The blood of Jesus keeps and guards
my mind day and night.
The blood of Jesus prevents deception
and aborts every attempt of the enemy to deceive me.
The blood of Jesus is my divine covering
and protection against all the fiery darts of the evil one.
Yea, the blood of Jesus is alive!
So full of life and grace it perfects
that which concerneth me -
reconciling everything in me to the perfect
will of God everyday and in every day.

- Grace Ryerson Roos

MAINTAIN

201

The Conquered Curse

Christ has redeemed me from the curse of the law,
As He hung on that shameful tree,
And all that is worse is contained in the curse,
And Jesus has set me free.

Refrain:
Not under the curse, not under the curse,
Jesus has set me free;
For sickness, I've health; for poverty, wealth,
Since Jesus has ransomed me.

Christ paid the price of the broken law,
He paid the whole price for me;
God saw not one spot, one blemish or blot,
In the Lamb that was slain for me.

Do not abide in the ancient days,
Ere ever the Lamb was slain;
Take that which was given as freely as heaven,
And join in the glad refrain.

- Lilian B. Yeoman

MARK AND TRINA HANKINS travel nationally and internationally preaching the Word of God with the power of the Holy Spirit. Their message centers on the spirit of faith, who the believer is in Christ, and the work of the Holy Spirit.

After over 50 years of pastoral and traveling ministry, Mark and Trina are now ministering full-time in camp-meetings, leadership conferences, and church services around the world and across the United States.

Their son, Aaron and his wife Errin Cody, are now the pastors of Christian Worship Center in Alexandria, Louisiana. Their daughter, Alicia Moran and her husband Caleb, live in Lafayette, Louisiana. Mark and Trina also have eight grandchildren.

For more information on Mark Hankins Ministries, please log on to our website, www.markhankins.org.

Special thanks to my sister, Ladelle Peabody, for the beautiful music accompaniment for the Healing Scriptures and Confession CD that go with this book.

Acknowledgements

I would like to express my gratitude to my husband, Mark Hankins who has fueled my faith since I met him. His example and leadership have guided me to victory in many areas of life. My parents, Bill and Ginger Behrman and Mark's parents, B.B. and Velma Hankins, along with Rev. K.E. Hagin have led us in the paths leading to the blessing of God, which includes prosperity in spirit, soul and body. I have this rich inheritance to pass to my children and grandchildren. Thank you, my wonderful Father for your goodness expressed through Jesus Christ. May your will for our health be done in the earth as it is in Heaven.

PURCHASING AND CONTACT INFORMATION:

MARK HANKINS MINISTRIES
PO BOX 12863
ALEXANDRIA, LA 71315

PHONE: 318.767.2001
FAX: 318.443.2948

E-MAIL: CONTACT@MARKHANKINS.ORG

VISIT US ON THE WEB:
WWW.MARKHANKINS.ORG

Mark Hankins Ministries Publications

SPIRIT-FILLED SCRIPTURE STUDY GUIDE

A comprehensive study of scriptures in over 120 different translations on topics such as: Redemption, Faith, Finances, Prayer and many more.

THE SPIRIT OF FAITH

If you only knew what was on the other side of your mountain, you would move it! Having a spirit of faith is necessary to do the will of God and fulfill your destiny.

THE BLOODLINE OF A CHAMPION - THE POWER OF THE BLOOD OF JESUS

The blood of Jesus is the liquid language of love that flows from the heart of God and gives us hope in all circumstances. In this book, you will clearly see what the blood has done FOR US but also what the blood has done IN US as believers.

TAKING YOUR PLACE IN CHRIST

Many Christians talk about what they are trying to be and what they are going to be. This book is about who you are NOW as a believer in Christ.

PAUL'S SYSTEM OF TRUTH

Paul's System of Truth reveals man's redemption in Christ, the reality of what happened from the cross to the throne and how it is applied for victory in life through Jesus Christ.

THE SECRET POWER OF JOY

If you only knew what happens in the Spirit when you rejoice, you would rejoice everyday! Joy is one of the great secrets of faith. This book will show you the importance of the joy of the Lord in a believes life!

11:23 - THE LANGUAGE OF FAITH

Never under–estimate the power of one voice! Over 100 inspirational, mountain-moving quotes to "stir–up" the spirit of faith in you.

ACKNOWLEDGING EVERY GOOD THING
THAT IS IN YOU IN CHRIST

This mini–book encourages every believer to have a daily confession or acknowledgment of who they are in Christ.

REVOLUTIONARY REVELATION

This book provides excellent insight on how the spirit of wisdom and revelation is mandatory for believers to access their call, inheritance, and authority in Christ.

LET THE GOOD TIMES ROLL

This book focuses on the five keys to heaven on earth: The Holy Spirit, Glory, Faith, Joy and Redemption. The Holy Spirit is a genius. If you will listen to Him, He will make you look smart.

www.markhankins.org

BIBLIOGRAPHY

The Bible Translations used in Section Two have the
abbreviations listed at the end of the reference

Adams, Jay E. *The New Testament in Everyday English.* Baker Book House, Grand Rapids, Michigan, 1979. (ADAMS)

A.J. Holman Company, New York, 1976.

American Standard Version. Thomas Nelson and Sons, New York 1901. (ASV)

Amplified Bible. Zondervan Publishing House, Grand Rapids, 1972. (AMP)

Barclay, William. *The Holy Bible of the Language of Today.* (BARCLAY)

Beck, William. *The Holy Bible in the Language of Today.* A.J. Holman Company, New York, New York, 1976. (BECK)

Bosworth, F.F. (1924). *Christ The Healer.* Grand Rapids, Michigan: Chosen Books Publishing Co.

Bounds, E.M. *The Best of EM Bounds.* Honor Books, September 2006.

Brenton, Charles Lee. *The Septuagint Version of the Old Testament.* Bagster Sons, London, England, 1944. (SEPT)

Breyer, M. Care2Make a Difference.

Byington, Stephen. *The Bible in Living English.* Watch Tower Bible and Tract Society of New York, 1972. (BYINGTON)

Catholic Public Domain Version. (BPDV)

Cho, David Yongii (2008), *Dreams and Vision* [DVD]. Baton Rouge, LA (October 8, 2008).

Colbert, D. (2003). *Deadly Emotions: Understand the Mind-Body-Spirit Connection That Can Heal or Destroy You.* Nashville, Tennessee: Thomas Nelson Publishing Co.

Common English Bible. Nashville, Tennessee, 2011. *Concordant Literal New Testament,* Sixth Edition. Concordant Publishing Concern, 1976. (CEB)

Condon, Kevin. *The Abba House New Testament.* The Priest And Brothers of the Society of St. Paul, New York, 1972. (CONDON)

Confraternity Version New Testament. Catholic Book Publishing Company, New York, New York, 1963. (CONF)

Contemporary English Version. American Bible Society. New York, NK, 1995. (CEV)

Conybeare, W.J. *The Epistles of Paul*. Marshall Morgan and Scott, London, n.d. (CONY)

Cuvek Translation. British & Foreign Bible Society, 1995. (CUVEK)

Deane, Anthony C. *St. Paul and His Letters*. Hodder and Stoughton, London England, n.d. (DEANE)

Douay-Rheims Version of the Holy Bible. Douay Bible House. New York, 1942. (DOUAY)

Feuer, Rabbi Aurohom Chaim, *Tehillim*. ArtScroll, Mesorah Publications, 1985.

Fenton, Ferrar. *The Holy Bible in Modern English*. Destiny Publisher, Massachusetts, n.d. (FENTON)

Gjerdingen, Dr. Dwenda. *The Network A Called Community of Women*.

Godbey, W.B. *Translation of The New Testament*. Newby Bookroom, Indiana, 1973. (GODBEY)

God's Word Translation. Baker Publishing Group, Grand Rapids, Michigan 1995 (GWT)

Good News Bible (Catholic Edition in Septuagint Order). British and Foreign Bible Society. (GNBDK)

Goodspeed, Edgar J. *The New Testament, An American Translation*. University of Chicago, Chicago, Illinois, 1923. (GSPD)

Hagin, K.E. *Healing Scriptures*. Faith Library Publications, Tulsa, OK, 2001.

Hagin, K.E. *I Believe in Visions*. Faith Library Publications, Tulsa, OK, 1984.

Hagin, K.E. *Steps to Answered Prayer*. Faith Library Publications, Tulsa, OK, 2003

Hayford, Jack. *Spirit-Filled Life Bible*. Thomas Nelson Inc, 2003.

Hooke, SH. *Bible in Basic English*. Cambridge University Press, 1965.

Institute for Scripture Research. The Scriptures 1998. (ISR98)

Jerusalem Bible. Double Day & Co., Inc. New York, 1968. (JER)

Johnson, Ben Campbell. *Matthew and Mark. A Rational Paraphrase of the New Testament*. Word Books, Waco, Texas, 1978. (JOHNSON)

Johnson, Ben Campbell. *The Heart of Paul. A Rational Paraphrase of the New Testament*. Word Books, Waco, Texas, 1976. (JOHNSON)

Jordan, Clarence. *The Cotton Patch Version of Paul's Epistles*. Association Press, New York, New York, 1968. (JORDAN)

Knox, Ronald. *The New Testament of Our Lord and Savior Jesus Christ, A New Translation.* Sheed and Ward, New York, New York, 1953. (KNOX)

Knox, Ronald. *The Old Testament Newly Translated from the Latin Vulgate.* Burns, Oates and Washbourne, Ltd., London, England, 1949. (KNOX)

Laubach, Frank C. *The Inspired Letters Clearest English.* Thomas Nelson & Sons, New York, 1956. (LAU)

Ledyard, Gleason. *The New Life Testament.* Word Books, Waco, Texas 1970. (NEW LIFE)

Leeser, Isaac. *Twenty-Four Books of the Holy Scriptures.* Hebrew Publishing Company, New York, n.d. (LEESER)

Lexhan English Bible. Logos Bible Software. 2010. (LEB)

Mabrey, Vicki and Sherwood, Roxanna. "Speaking in Tongues: Alternative Voices in Faith." http://abcnews.go.com/Nightline/story?id=2935819&page=1#. UXyNJJVgpPFJ, March 20, 2007.

Marshall, Alfred. *The Interlinar Greek- English New Testament.* Zondervan Publishing House, Grand Rapids, 1975. (MARSHALL)

Moffatt, James. *The Holy Bible Containing the Old and New Testament.* Double Day Dora & Company, Inc., New York, 1926. (MOF)

Montgomery, Helen Barrett. *Centenary Translation of the New Testament.* The American Baptist Publication Society, Philadelphia, Pennsylvania, 1924. (CENT)

Moore, Keith. "Rest of God" and "The Glory is Here", http://www.flcbranson.org/freedownloads-music.php.

New English Bible. Oxford University Press, Oxford, 1961. (NEB)

New English Translation. Biblical Studies Press, Dallas Texas, 2005. (NET)

New International Version of the Holy Bible. Zondervan Bible. Publishers, Grand Rapids, 1978. (NIV)

New Living Translation. Tyndale House Publishers. Wheaton, Illinois, 1996. (NLT)

New King James Version. Thomas Nelson and Sons, New York, New York, 1982. (NKJV)

Noah Webster's 1828 Dictionary, http://1828.mshaffer.com

Noli, Fan S. *The New Testament of Our Lord and Savior Jesus Christ.* Albania Orthodox Church in American, Boston, 1961. (NOLI)

Norlie, Olaf M. *Norlie's Simplified New Testament in Plain English – For Today's Readers.* Zondervan, Grand Rapids, Michigan, 1961. (NORLIE)

Orthadox Jewish Bible. Israel International, Inc. 2011. (OJB)

Osteen, Dodie. *Healed of Cancer.* Struik Christian Books, 1987.

Peterson, Dr. Carl. "Medical Facts About Speaking In Tongues" http://beingunderthenewcovenant.wordpress.com.

Peterson, Eugene. *The Message//Remix,* The Bible in Contemporary Language. NavPress Publishing Group, Colorado Springs, Colorado, 2003. (MSG)

Phillips, J.B. *The New Testament in Modern English.* The Macmillan Company, New York, New York, 1958 (PHIL)

Prince, Jospeph, http://vitaminforthesoul.blogspot.com/2008/04/jesus-bore-your-diseases.html.

Revised Standard Version. Thomas Nelson and Sons, New York, New York, 1952. (RSV)

Rieu, E.VV. *The Acts of the Apostles.* Penguin Books, London, England, 1957. (RIEV)

Rieu, E.VV. *The Four Gospels.* Penguin Books, London, England, 1953 (RIEV)

Rotherham, J.B. *The Emphasized Bible.* Kregel Publications, Grand Rapids, Michigan, 1976. (ROTH)

Samuel Rolles Driver. (October 2, 1846- February 26, 1914).

Schonfield, Hugh. *The Authentic New Testament.* Dennis Dobson, Ltd., Great Britain, 1955. (AUTHENTIC)

Simpson, A.B. *The Gospel of Healing.* New York, New York: Christian Alliance Publishing Co, 1890.

Strong, James. The New Strong Exhaustive Concordance of the Bible, G2983, G4982, H5526, H8426.

Taylor, John. *A Paraphrase with Notes on the Epistles to the Romans.* J. Waugh, London, England, 1974. (TAYLOR)

Taylor, Ken. *The Living Bible.* Tyndale House Publishers. Wheaton, Illinois, 1971. (TLB)

Tehillim, Mesorah Publication, Inc., 1977.

The Abbreviated Bible. Van Nostrand, New York, New York, n.d. (ABBREV BIBLE)

The Bible in Basic English. University Press, Cambridge, England, 1965 (BASIC)

The Distilled Bible/New Testament. Paul Benjamin Publishing Company, Stone Mountain, Georgia, 1980. (DIST)

The Holy Scriptures. A New Testament, The Jewish Publications Society of American, Philadelphia, 1917. (MASORETIC O.T.)

The Jerusalem Bible. Double Day and Company, Inc., New York, New York, 1968. (JER.)

The Translator's New Testament. The British and Foreign Bible Society, London, England, 1977. (TRANS)

The Twentieth Century New Testament. The Fleming H. Revell Company, New York, New York, 1902. (20TH CR)

Wade, G.W. *The Documents of the New Testament.* Thomas Burby and Company, London, England, 1934. (WADE)

Wand, J.W.C. *The New Testament Letters.* Oxford University Press, Oxford, England, 1946. (WAND)

Way, Arthur S. *The Letters of St. Paul to the Seven Churches and Three Friends with the Letter to the Hebrews,* Sixth Edition. Macmillian and Company, New York, New York, 1926. (WAY)

Webster's 1828 Dictionary. http://1828.mshaffer.com/d/search/word,gratitude

Weymouth, Richard Francis. *The New Testament.* James Clark and Company, London, England, 1909. (WEYM)

Williams, Charles Kingsley. *The New Testament, A New Translation in Plain English.* Longmans, Green, and Co., London, England, 1952. (PL. ENGLISH)

Worrell, A.S. *The Worrell New Testament.* Gospel Publishing House, Springfield, Missouri, 1980. (WORRELL)

Wuest, Kenneth S. *The New Testament, An Expanded Translation.* William B. Eerdmans Publishing Company, Grand Rapids, Michigan, 1981. (WUEST)

VerHulst, Don. *10 Keys that Cure.* Don VerHulst, 2008.

Verkuyl, Gerrit. *The Holy Bible, The Berkeley Version in Modern English.* Zondervan Publishing House, Grand Rapids, Michigan, 1959. (BERKLEY)

Young, Arthur. *Young's Literal Translation of the Holy Bible.* (YOUNG)